European Festivals

Songs, dances, and customs from around Europe

Jean Gilbert

Acknowledgements

I am indebted to many people who have helped with this collection.

Spain

Fifina Gailey, formerly Maria-Josefa Alburquerque Lorencio, now a teacher of Spanish dancing, introduced me to the songs and dances, translated the verses and taught me the dance arrangements. I thank her for her many valuable suggestions, including craft work and costume.

Greece

Maria Merodoulaki, formerly a dancer in Crete and dance teacher at the Lykion Ton Hellinidon in London, taught me the dances 'Kastorianos' and 'Repati', suggested the accompaniments `that she uses in her own teaching and helped with translation.

Helen Galatis kindly gave permission for the inclusion of 'Lénim `thi Mais'. This beautiful dance was collected by her mother Lillian Galatis who arranged and described it in her book *Ten Simple Greek Folk `Dances*.

p.27 Easter buns from *International Cook Book* © 1982, Paul Hamlyn.

Bulgaria

Dr Mercia MacDermott, an authority on Bulgarian history and author of several noted books, generously supplied notes, recipes, songs with translations, suggestions for craftwork and costume sketches that enabled me to complete this section.
I am most grateful.

Professor Dimiter Christoff sent me the song 'Kralyo portalyo' from Sofia.

Brian Dowsett, member of the Dunav Balkan Group, taught me the dance 'Pravo trakijsko horo'.

Hungary

József Baracsi, leader of the Hungarian Folk Dance Group (London), contributed the song dances, translations, the 'Pogácsa' recipe, ideas for art work and notes on costume. I thank him for our working sessions when I learnt the dances and many facts about Hungarian history and customs.

Czech Republic

Hedy Fromings, leader of the Beskydy Dancers and teacher of Czech and Slovak dances, provided material for the songs, dances and costume illustrations, taught me the dances and translated the songs. I thank her for her consistent support.

p.60 Recipes from *Come and Enjoy the Czechoslovak Cuisine* © Merkur for Ministry of Trade and Tourism, Prague.

Germany

Barbara Lester, lecturer and researcher, kindly brought songs from Germany and translated the verses.

p.73 Imitation lantern elaborated from *The Children's Year* by Stephanie Cooper, Christine Ffynes-Clinton and Marye Rowling, Hawthorn Press, 1 Lansdown Lane, Stroud, Gloucester GL5 1BJ, UK 1986.

France

Francine Ducarre, teacher at the French School in London sent me material. Maryvonne Potts, teacher at the Lycée Français in London, suggested the songs from Brittany, outlined the dance arrangements for 'La Carmagnole' and helped with the translations.

Sweden

Maria Ericsson of the Swedish Church in London suggested the song dances for this section, taught me the dances and translated the verses.

p.97–98 Recipes and Dalecarlion Horse kindly supplied by the Swedish Embassy. Source: *Delicious Swedish Food*, published by Lilla Sällskapet.

I have also gathered material from many other sources. I acknowledge the help of officials from the Embassies who have answered questions, sent me much information and read through the manuscript. Of the many books I have consulted, I would like to mention in particular 'Folk Costumes of the World' and 'Aspects of Folk Dance in Europe' (see General reference), which I found especially helpful when preparing descriptions of the costumes.

p.113 Dance instructions used by permission of Novello & Co.

Special thanks are due to Pauline Woloshin and Leslie Gilbert for their encouragement and critical support throughout the project and to Chris Wood, my editor, for pulling everything together.

To all who have contributed, I offer my sincere thanks. I have learnt such a lot and I hope the children will too.

Designed and typeset by Cox Design Partnership, Witney, Oxford.

Black and white illustrations by Adrian Barclay and Kathy Baxendale.

Colour section and cover illustration by Derek Lockhart.

Oxford University Press, Great Clarendon Street, Oxford OX2 6DP
Oxford New York
Athens Auckland Bangkok Bogota Bombay Buenos Aires
Calcutta Cape Town Dar es Salaam Delhi Florence Hong Kong
Istanbul Karachi Kuala Lumpur Madras Madrid Melbourne
Mexico City Nairobi Paris Singapore Taipei Tokyo Toronto Warsaw
and associated companies in Berlin Ibadan

Oxford is a trade mark of Oxford University Press

© Jean Gilbert 1997

10 9 8 7 6 5 4 3 2 1

Printed in Hong Kong

Contents

List of CD tracks

The CD is inserted inside the back cover
This page may be photocopied

Spain: Fifina Gailey (speaker and castanets), Barry Mason (guitar), Glenda Simpson (singer), Andrew Veivers (guitar). *Greece:* Sofia Charalambous (speaker, keyboard, singer), Dunav Balkan Group (dance accompaniment), Nick Efthymiou (bouzouki), Lilija Zobens (singer). *Bulgaria:* Dunav Balkan Group (dance accompaniment), Vanya Getova (speaker), Lilija Zobens (singer). *Hungary:* Jean Gilbert (piano), Gyula Gaspár (zither), Zsuzsanna Hinton (speaker and singer), Janos Hosszu (violin). *Czech Republic:* Beskydy Dancers Musicians (accompaniment), Hedy Fromings (speaker and singer). *Germany:* Jean Gilbert (piano and glockenspiel), Mike Ruff (accordion), Renate Wendel (speaker and singer). *France:* Joëlle Chaine (singer), Nathalie Dejonghe (speaker), Mike Ruff (accordion). *Sweden:* Mike Ruff (accordion), Lisa Wiktorssons (speaker and singer). *May Day:* Carolyn Robson (singer), Mike Ruff (accordion).

Recorded at Pathway Studios, London. Edited at Mark Angelo Recording Studios, London.

Introduction

Whatever the political arrangements, the cultural and historical links of the United Kingdom with the rest of Europe are becoming increasingly important to us and to our children. The ease of modern travel is also strengthening our ties with the Continent. At the educational level the importance of these links has been recognized through the policy of encouraging schools to make what is called the 'European dimension', part of the curriculum.

This book and CD aim to support schools that wish to bring a flavour of Europe into the classroom. Through the songs, dances, cooking, craft and language activities the children can begin to experience and therefore appreciate the culture of a number of countries, both inside and outside the European Union.

Festivals have often left cultural marks and can sometimes help to give a better 'feel' of a country than a purely factual description. The celebration of special days or particular events has always been important to the people of Europe. Their festivals are deeply rooted in the histories and cultures of their countries, as are the songs and dances associated with them. Some festivals such as France's 'Le 14 Juillet' have arisen comparatively recently. Others, May Day for instance, date back thousands of years. Despite the sophistication of modern life, festivals are still celebrated, especially outside the larger urban areas. A number of them, some with their songs and dances, are described in the country sections.

At the moment there is very little available material organized in a way that would be of practical use to the busy teacher. Perhaps this is not surprising, for it is widely scattered and difficult to track down. However I hope that the results of my search will provide a wide variety of activities which the children can enjoy and which will stimulate a desire to find out more about life among our European neighbours.

The European dimension

The Department for Education and Employment has outlined the policy in respect of The European dimension in Education. It advocates 'helping pupils to acquire a view of Europe as a multicultural, multilingual community which includes the UK' and 'encouraging awareness of the variety of European histories, geographies and cultures (including the languages)'. The National Curriculum provides a framework for integrating the European dimension into the curriculum by linking aspects of it to the statutory requirements of individual subjects. Specific references to European matters are made in the curricula for Geography, History, Modern Foreign Languages, Art and Music. The Department's guidance advises that the European dimension also needs to be part of a school's whole curriculum policy. This publication will be a valuable curriculum resource in this context.

How the book is organized

There are eight countries represented. The material for each includes:

- a brief historical and geographical background of the country (which may be photocopied), written in a style for children to read for themselves. It is assumed that the selective information will be amplified by the teacher as necessary.
- useful words and phrases in the language of the country;
- information about food and meals, with simple recipes for the children to try;
- ideas for art/craft activities;
- festival or regional songs and dances;
- resource lists of useful books, addresses, and recorded music, both classical and folk;
- colour illustrations of folk costumes in the centre of the book.

In addition, there is a section on May Day. It describes the various European customs associated with this ancient festival, and outlines the May Day traditions at Padstow and Helston in England.

How the book can be used

- For a study of one country linked to work in geography or history;
- For a project on language, including a general study of European languages, a comparative study of the names of numbers; or a comparison of common words;
- For a project on food;
- For general art and craft activities, or linked to a topic such as costume;
- For music and movement activities.

The CD

There is an intimate connection between the culture of a country and its language, as the statement on the European dimension in Education recognizes in its reference to a 'multicultural, multilingual community'. That is why this book has a substantial multilingual content. However, a language consists of much more than written words. Words come alive and attain their proper cultural significance only when they are spoken or sung in relevant contexts. And we must not forget that music, for example of a song or dance, is also a language, one that (especially in the case of traditional music) has deep roots in its country's cultural development.

The CD that accompanies this book has therefore been conceived as an integral part of *European Festivals*, to help the teacher to make the most effective use of the language material, the songs and the dances included in the book.

The sign ② indicates that the item is on the accompanying CD, and the number refers to the CD track. A cassette copy may be made of part or all of the CD for educational purposes only by the purchaser of the book and CD. Multiple copies may not be made, and no copies may be sold.

The language material

The book introduces a few simple words, singly and in phrases, in each language, together with language activities and games to help the children use the words meaningfully. The children will first need to be able to pronounce them, and to recognize them when heard. Phonetic transcriptions and pronunciation guides are not always reliable or helpful, especially in the less familiar languages. The words are therefore spoken at an appropriate speed on the recording at the beginning of the section for each country. The children should practise repeating them until they are sufficiently familiar with the pronunciation to be able to take part in the activities and games.

The songs

It is strongly recommended that the songs are sung in their original languages, and as far as possible in their correct styles. It is only in this way that the children will really experience their full flavour and cultural uniqueness. These are qualities that the recorded performances aim to illustrate. To help the children to follow the recordings, and then to attempt their own performances, the words are spoken clearly, and in the correct pronunciation, before being sung.

The book includes English versions of the song lyrics. They are not literal translations, but are intended to convey the sense of the content and to allow the children to learn them in English. The main concern has been to fit the stress of the words with that of the music, with rhyme as a secondary feature.

The dances

The recordings aim to reflect, as far as possible, the 'sound' of the music of the different countries. Keyboard arrangements are given in the book. The music can also be used for some of the games.

General classroom activities

Topic work

These suggestions provide ideas for topic work connected with European countries. They apply to each of the countries presented. Activities that are specific to one country are outlined in that section.

- Collect pictures, postcards, books and illustrations about the country and make a display.
- Ask a child, parent or friend who has been to the country, or lived there, to tell the class about their visit or stay. Have they any photos, videos, souvenirs or music cassettes from the country that the class could look at or listen to?
- Ask the children to find items in British newspapers about the country. Is there a foreign newspaper in the language?
- Show the children how to find foreign radio stations. Can they find a station where the language is being spoken or sung?
- Look for items of food or other products in the local shops. Collect labels and containers to make a display.
- Prepare some simple meals or snacks with ideas from the recipe sections. Interested parents, especially those from the country concerned, may have more ideas. Invite them in to help.

- Teach some numbers and phrases in the language from the recording. There are suggestions for games on page 7.
- Read some folk tales, legends or traditional stories from the country. Discuss them with the children. What do they tell them about the country? Children can make and illustrate a class story book.
- Find out more about folk costumes. There are many different regional costumes in each country. The children might like to make a collage of figures, using ideas from the centre colour section, or other pictures they have obtained.
- Invite parents or children from another class to an open afternoon. The children can tell them what they have found out about the country, sing some songs and show examples of the dances.

Number games

When the children are familiar with the numbers 1 to 10 in a chosen language, play some of the following games. It is best to start with a few numbers and gradually extend. Prepare two sets of cards, one with digits ('number cards') and one with words ('word cards').

Number match 1 (small group)

- Give a number card to each child.
- Say a number in the chosen language.
- Any child who has the correct card holds it up and says the number in the language (e.g. 'deux', not 'two').

Number match 2 (small group)

- Play the game as for 'Number match 1', this time using word cards. The number could be said either in the chosen language or in English. Encourage one of the children to lead the group.

Number bumps (class or group)

Play this game in the hall or a large space where the children can move about.

- Give every child a number card.
- Play the music of one of the dances of the chosen country. The children walk or dance around freely and stop when the music stops.
- Say clearly one of the numbers in the chosen language. All the children with that number sit down; the last one is 'out'. Anyone who sits down by mistake, or who fails to sit down is also 'out'.
- Continue until you have a winner.

Circle game 1 (class or group)

- Sit the children in a circle. Practise saying the numbers in the chosen language first. Put some number cards in the centre, face down.
- The children pass a beanbag round while they sing the first verse of a song (either in the chosen language or in English) or clap to the music of one of the dances.
- The child with the beanbag at the end of the verse, or when the music stops, picks up a card from the centre and calls out the number in the chosen language.
- The game proceeds; there are no winners.

Circle game 2 (class or group)

This is a variation of Circle game 1.

- Put an instrument, e.g. drum or tambourine, in the middle of the circle.
- Proceed as before, passing the beanbag around.
- When the music or verse stops, call out a number in the chosen language. The child with the beanbag has to respond by playing the corresponding number of beats on the instrument.
- A leader can be chosen to start the game off and call out the numbers.

Missing number (group)

- Put a few number cards in the middle of the circle.
- Let the children practise saying the relevant numbers in the chosen language, first together, then individually.
- Say all the numbers except one.
- The children call out the name of the missing number, or within a reasonably small group, the first one to pick up the missing number wins.

Number snap (groups of two or three)

- Deal a pack of number cards in the usual way as for the game 'Snap'.
- The usual rules apply, except that the players say the number in the chosen language instead of the word 'snap'.
- It is a good idea to have a referee!

Word games

Practise the words and phrases in the chosen language.

Word match (small group)

- Prepare a set of cards with the words written in the chosen language.
- Give a card to each child.
- Say one of the words in the chosen language.
- Any child with a matching card holds it up and says the word.
- Repeat the activity, saying the words in English. The children respond as before, holding up the correct card and saying the word in the language.
- Encourage one of the children to lead the group.

Conversations (class or group)

This game introduces the children to the phrases in a particular language.

- Give the children access to the relevant page in this book of the language they would like to practise. Let them make up mini-conversations from the phrases and 'perform' them in the chosen language. (This is a good exercise in roleplaying.) E.g.

Rosie:	Good morning *or* good afternoon
Ahmed:	Good morning *or* good afternoon
Rosie:	How are things?
Ahmed:	Fine, thanks
Rosie:	Goodbye
Ahmed:	Goodbye

Encourage the children to use the words during the day: 'Good morning', when they come in, 'Goodbye', when they leave and 'yes'/'no' and 'please'/'thank you' whenever they can amongst themselves and during class activities.

The vocabulary of these activities could be extended if you or the children or their parents are familiar with the chosen language.

Calendar of festivals and customs

		General reference page	Activity page
JANUARY			
New Year (Súrva) (1st)	Bulgaria	44	43
FEBRUARY			
Carnival (Fasching)	Germany	73	
MARCH			
Martenítsa (1st)	Bulgaria	44	42–43
Liberation Day (Den na Osvobozhdenieto na Bălgarija) (3rd)	Bulgaria	40	
Las Fallas (19th)	Spain	15	
Independence Day (Epanastassi tou 1821) (25th)	Greece	30	37–38
APRIL			
Lazaruvané	Bulgaria	44	44–45
Death Sunday (Smrtná neděla)	Czech Republic	62	62
Easter (Velikonoce)	Czech Republic	61	
Easter (húsvét)	Hungary	53	53
April Fair (Feria de abril)	Spain	15	
Spring festivals (Frühlingsfest)	Germany		75–77
Procession to the Alps (Almauftrieb)	Germany	73	
El Bando de la huerta	Spain	15	18
Walpurgis Night (Valborgsmässoafton) (30th)	Sweden	99	
MAY			
May Day (1st) General		105	
(Protomaya)	Greece	30	
(Le Premier Mai)	France	85	
(májusfaállitás)	Hungary	53	
(Svátek práce)	Czech Republic	62	
	Britain	105–106	106–115
Whitsun (pünkösd)	Hungary	53	55
The Day of Bulgarian Education and Culture (Kiril i Metodi) (24th)	Bulgaria	40	
JUNE			
Festival of Roses (Festival na Rozata)	Bulgaria	39	
Midsummer (Midsommar) (24th)	Sweden	97	99–104
JULY			
Los Sanfermines (7th)	Spain	15	21
Feast of Wheat (arató ünnep)	Hungary	53	
Bastille Day (Le 14 Juillet) (14th)	France	81	85–90
Marksmen's Festivals (Schützenfeste)	Germany	73	
AUGUST			
La Semana grande (15th)	Spain		22–24
St. Stephen's Day (20th)	Hungary	50	
SEPTEMBER			
October Fair (Oktoberfest)	Germany	73	
Grape Harvest (szüret)	Hungary	53	
Return from Mountain Pastures (Almabtrieb)	Germany	73	
OCTOBER			
Ohi Day (Imera tou Ohi) (28th)	Greece	30	37–38
NOVEMBER			
St Martin's Festival (Martinfest) (11th)	Germany	74	73-74
DECEMBER			
Lucia Day (Luciadagen) (13th)	Sweden	99	
Christmas (Karácsony) (25th)	Hungary	53	
(Noël) (25th)	France	85	

Spain

España

Spain is one of Europe's largest and most mountainous countries, a land of great dramatic contrasts.

The most well known parts of Spain are probably the Mediterranean seaside resorts on the Costas (coasts) where many thousands of tourists spend their summer holidays. But much of Spain is very different from these hot, sandy beaches with their tall, white hotels.

In the north it is green and rainy. Rocky coasts face the Atlantic Ocean, and further inland the land is quite wild, mountainous and very sparsely populated. The great mountain range of the Pyrenees in the north-east forms a natural border with France. There are heavy snowfalls in winter and the buildings have steep sided roofs so that the snow will slide off.

Further south, inland Spain is covered by a high central plateau known as the Meseta, which means 'tableland'. Here the climate is at its most extreme. In Madrid, the capital, which is right in the centre, summers are very hot but winters are bitterly cold. The vast, dry plain near Toledo is usually very windy too. There are many windmills that have been used for centuries to grind wheat and barley, though some have now been converted into rather breezy homes. The old kingdom of Castile is famous as the setting of Cervantes' novel, *Don Quixote*.

The sunny climate is good for growing fruit and vegetables. Oranges and orange juice drinks such as Fanta are among Spain's chief exports. Our breakfast marmalade is made from Seville oranges which are bitter and until recently disliked in Spain! Olive oil and wine are also major exports. Sherry takes its name from the city of Jerez de la Frontera, well known to wine merchants for centuries.

History

The early history of Spain is a story of invasions and settlements of people from other countries over thousands of years.

Iberians from North Africa, traders from Greece and Carthage and Celtic people from north of the Pyrenees settled in Spain before it became part of the great Roman Empire.

In AD 711, Moors and Arabs from North Africa invaded and ruled over most of Spain for almost 800 years. They built beautiful palaces such as the Alhambra in Granada. Cordoba, their capital, became one of the most splendid and important cities in Europe. Their rule ended when they were defeated by the Christian armies of Ferdinand and Isabella in 1492. In the same year, Christopher Columbus crossed the Atlantic and 'discovered' the West Indies. Spain became rich and powerful from her new colonies in Central and South America. Spanish is still the third most widely spoken language in the world today.

Slowly the power of Spain began to decline. The great Spanish fleet, the Armada, was defeated by the English in 1588. Further costly wars followed and by 1824 most of the colonies in America had broken free from Spanish rule.

In the present century a terrible civil war (1936–39) caused great suffering among the people. It ended when General Franco took over as dictator. After Franco's death in 1975, Juan Carlos de Bourbon became king, and Spain returned to democratic rule.

Language

Castilian, the language spoken in central Spain, is what is generally regarded as Spanish. It belongs to the Romance group of languages derived from Latin and is one of the largest languages in the world.

English	Spanish
one	uno
two	dos
three	tres
four	cuatro
five	cinco
six	seis
seven	siete
eight	ocho
nine	nueve
ten	diez
good morning	buenos dias
good afternoon	buenas tardes
good evening	buenas noches
hello	hola
how are things?	¿qué tal?
fine	bien
thank you	gracias
please	por favor
yes	sí
no	no
goodbye	adiós

Suggestions for language activities can be found on page 7.

Food and drink

Food is an important part of life in Spain and is as varied as the country itself. Local markets with their colourful displays of fruit, vegetables and local produce are still popular even though there are now supermarkets.

One of the most famous of Spanish dishes is named after the large pan in which it is cooked. Paella is based on rice cooked with chicken and every available type of sea food. The best version is said to come from Valencia. Equally well known is the tortilla, a potato omelette cooked on both sides and eaten hot or cold. Families or groups of friends eating out in taverns like to order one tortilla large enough for everyone to share. It is served with bread rolls, tomatoes and jugs of wine and all tuck in!

Andalusia, a leading olive growing region, uses the oil to prepare gazpacho. This cold refreshing soup is just right for sweltering summer days. But the national dish which is found all over Spain is the cocido, a hearty stew consisting of meat, pulses and vegetables, whatever is typical of the area.

Because of the midday heat in summer, Spaniards eat much later than we do here. Lunch does not start until about 2 pm and is often the main meal of the day. It is common for people to take a 'siesta' before returning to work at about 4 pm. Dinner is not until 9.30 pm at the earliest or even later at weekends. In between children may have a tea-time snack, and before dinner people visit tapas bars where little snacks ('tapas') such as dry cured ham, olives, anchovies or slices of tortilla are served. This is the time for the nightly 'paseo' when people stroll around looking at shop windows and greeting friends and neighbours.

Tortilla de patatas (Spanish omelette)

3 eggs	1 small onion
2 medium sized potatoes	oil
	pinch of salt

Chop up the onion and fry till golden.

Peel and finely chop the potatoes and fry gently in covered pan until tender but not crisp.

Sieve onions and potatoes to drain out any excess fat.

Add the well-beaten eggs to the onions and potatoes, mix well, season to taste and fry.

Turn over by slipping onto a plate or lid and returning to reoiled pan to cook on the other side.

All Spanish omelettes are served flat, not rolled.

Gazpacho (Cold vegetable soup)

1kg large ripe tomatoes
2 small cloves garlic
2 slices (decrusted) bread
1 green pepper (deseeded)
salt to taste
3 tablespoons olive oil
3 tablespoons wine vinegar
3 tablespoons water
1 cup ice cubes

Mix the vinegar and water and pour over the crumbled bread.

Wash, peel and cut up the tomatoes and put them into a blender with the sliced garlic and pepper.

Add the oil and soaked bread and blend into a thick purée.

Pour out, add ice cubes and let it stand.

Season to taste.

Serve with finely diced green pepper, onion, cucumber and tiny cubes of toasted bread or 'croutons'.

A very simple gazpacho can be made with a can of tomato juice blended with the juice of a lemon, 2 tablespoons of wine vinegar, seasoned and served with finely diced vegetables as above.

Further suggestions

- A few cold tortillas could form the basis for a 'tapas' spread. Add some portions of cooked food such as slices of meat with olives, small pieces of cooked fish, little salads, cheese dips etc.
- Prepare a light Spanish type school lunch using the above recipes.
- See 'General classroom activities' on page 6.

Some famous people

Music

Composers include
Albeniz (1860–1909)
Granados (1867–1916)
and Falla (1876–1946)

World-famous performers include
Montserrat Caballé
(1933–) soprano
Victoria de los Angeles
(1923–) soprano
Placido Domingo
(1941–) tenor
and Andrés Segovia
(1894–1987) guitarist

The Gaudi cathedral in Barcelona

Art and architecture

Famous painters include
El Greco (1541–1614)
Velazquez (1599–1660)
Murillo (1618–82)
Goya (1746–1828)
Picasso (1881–1973)
and Dali (1904–89)

Gaudi (1852–1926) was an **architect** who was inspired by nature. His cathedral of Sagrada Familia in Barcelona is a landmark in the city.

Literature

Cervantes (1547–1616) was a literary genius whose novel *Don Quixote* has been translated and read by people all over the world.

Traditional culture

The art form most associated with the spirit of Spain is that of 'flamenco', the traditional wild and beautiful singing and dancing of the Andalusian Gypsies. Although performances are centred around the singing, it is the dancers with their intricate footwork and staccato stamping who often capture the audience. The only accompaniment is the guitar, shouts of 'Olé!' and the rhythmic hand clapping.

Bullfighting has been popular in Spain since Roman times. Although it is regarded as cruel in many countries, in Spain it is seen as part of a cultural tradition and an art requiring great skill.

Main crops:

barley, wheat, sugar beet, vegetables, fruit, fish

People's jobs:

Agricultural	10%
Industrial	32%
Other	58%

Main industries:

cars, shipbuilding, chemicals, steel, textiles, footwear

Art and craft

Spain is noted for its leather goods, especially shoes, ceramics and, of course, fans.

Here are suggestions for making simple fans from stiff coloured paper or thin card.

Cut out shapes from the sides if you want to create a lacy effect.

Decorate the fan before you start by painting or colouring patterns or pictures. Attractive wallpaper will make an interesting fan

Pinch or secure one end of a piece of pleated paper and open out the fan.

Make paper windmills and attach to a small stick or to improvised Spanish windmills.

Suggestions for general classroom activities can be found on page 6.

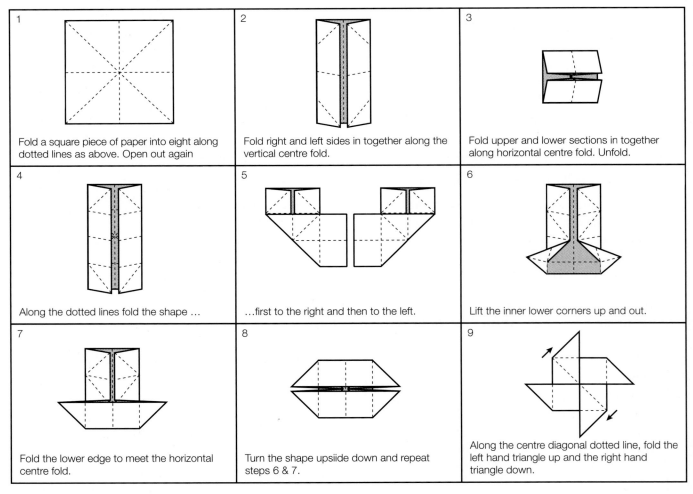

1	2	3
Fold a square piece of paper into eight along dotted lines as above. Open out again	Fold right and left sides in together along the vertical centre fold.	Fold upper and lower sections in together along horizontal centre fold. Unfold.
4	5	6
Along the dotted lines fold the shape …	…first to the right and then to the left.	Lift the inner lower corners up and out.
7	8	9
Fold the lower edge to meet the horizontal centre fold.	Turn the shape upsiide down and repeat steps 6 & 7.	Along the centre diagonal dotted line, fold the left hand triangle up and the right hand triangle down.

Fix the windmill to a stick with a pin or small nail.   OR   Improvise a Spanish type windmill from thick card (see page 11). Attach the paper sails at the top.

Folk costume

Spain has a wealth of costumes and a great variety of styles. In general the costumes from the mountain areas of the north are simple and austere, whereas those of the south are richer and more colourful. Skirts are full and gathered and in most regions shawls are worn. Men wear knee breeches, often worn loosely over white under-trousers ('pololos'), or trousers which, in Andalusia, are very tight-fitting up to the waist and worn with a short waistcoat. Head-dresses for women are simple, a kerchief or just a flower; men wear brimmed hats in the south against the sun, or berets, turbans or stocking caps in other areas. Shoes can be firm with a heel or flat like the rope-soled 'alpargatas' popular in the south. The costumes illustrated in the colour section are from Murc

Here are some ideas for a simple Spanish type costume for dressing up on special occasions, or even just for fun and extra interest when dancing (see illustration).

Girls Black leotard with any coloured calf length flouncy skirt. Big ear-rings and a flower in the hair. A coloured neck fringe to match the skirt looks good.

Boys Black trousers with a red band tied round the waist or with the shirt tied around the middle and a coloured neck scarf.

Any shoes will do but an authentic touch would be heeled shoes like tap shoes, preferably leather.

Festivals

All over Spain there are festivals or fiestas throughout the year, many with strong religious origins. 'Verbenas' are town fiestas held in honour of a saint, while in the country, village pilgrimages called 'romerías' are made to the shrine of the local Patron Saint. Holy Week is observed throughout the country when statues from the churches are paraded through the streets.

Bonfires to celebrate the day of St Joseph, the Patron Saint of carpenters, take place on March 19 at the end of a week of fireworks and feasting. It is thought that the ritual of burning wood shavings and sawdust on this day originated in the sixteenth century. Today, Valencia is famed for its huge papier mâché giants, 'las Fallas', which are up to 9 metres tall. These figures, usually satirical portrayals of well known people or famous events, are constructed throughout the year by local carpenters and artists. All except the one judged to be the best are torched, lighting up the sky over the city.

Bullfighting is popular in the south of Spain and bulls are also at the very heart of many celebrations. The best known is probably Los Sanfermines, the famous bull fiesta at Pamplona in honour of the Patron Saint, San Fermín, when young bulls are let loose in the crowded streets (see 'Canción de San Fermín' on page 21).

The conquest of the Moors by the Christians is celebrated in many places with mock battles, processions and ancient dances. The April Fair ('Feria de abril') of Seville, with its horse parades and beautiful costumes of the women, is one of Spain's most picturesque fiestas. Here, in the south, flamenco music and dance are part of the traditional festivities.

The following dance (page 16), a 'jota', comes from Murcia. It is danced in the streets by everyone during the fiesta of El Bando de la huerta, which is part of the Spring festivals, and takes place during the week following Easter. The province of Murcia is called 'el Jardín de Europa' ('the Garden of Europe'). It is one of the driest parts of Spain but it has stretches of fertile soil and rivers whose waters irrigate three crops in succession each year. Most of Spain's fruit and vegetable exports come from Murcia.

During the fiesta, farmers from surrounding districts bring their crops into the town and take part in big processions and parades. As the festival spirit takes over, some of the crops become part of a traditional game as they are thrown high into the air to land among the onlookers!

Jota de Murcia

Traditional tune
Accompaniment adapted from Marilyn Swinn

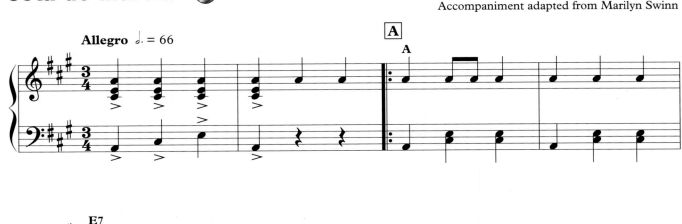

CODA ⊕

The dance

The 'Jota de Murcia' is a partner dance. When the children are ready they can perform it in groups of four (see 1).

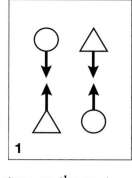

Introduction — Take 4 turning steps opposite partner.

A music — 16 quick waltz steps on the spot, facing partner, starting to the right. Arms at shoulder level stretch over to the right, then over to the left as the leading foot changes (see 2).

2 R.L.R.   L.R.L.

B music — 12 jota steps (see below). Face partner and both begin with the right foot.

A music — Partners pass one another back to back with 8 quick waltz steps and return to places with 8 more waltz steps.

B music — 12 jota steps as before.

A music — Partners stand alongside one another with right shoulders adjacent and the left (outside) arm raised in a curve. They circle right with 8 quick waltz steps and with head turned to look at their partner, then return, circling left with right arm raised, to places. Finish with a final stamp!

The jota step (see 3)

bar 1 Point right foot diagonally right and hold for 1 bar (3 beats).

bar 2 Quick hop on left as right foot steps back. Left foot steps to the side and right foot steps across and forward. The left foot is now ready to point diagonally left to start the next step to return to place.
(Left, hold for 1 bar, left, right, left . . .)
Each jota step lasts for 2 bars.

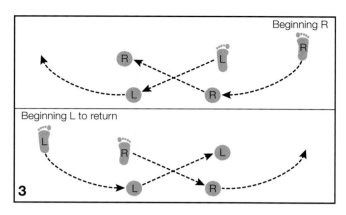

The arms are curved with the 'leading' arm at hip level and the other arm higher at head level. They change as the 'leading' foot changes.

Jota step variation

When the children are familiar with the step described above they could try a simple variation. Instead of travelling to the side and back again, they could go away from their partner (with a backward turn) and back again.

Teaching the dance

Introduce the quick waltz step first, slowing it down to the speed that the children can manage. Let the children practise it both on the spot and in motion, making their own movement patterns. When they are ready, speed it up and introduce the formations described for the A music.

Similarly introduce the jota step. Try it on the spot first and leave out the hop so that the movements are: right foot forward for 3 beats (weight on left), step RLR, left foot forward for 3 beats (weight on right), step LRL and so on. When the children are ready, speed up their practice and introduce the movements described for the jota step.

Costume

See page 15 for simple ideas for dressing up with a Spanish look. For this jota, girls can wear hand ribbons. These consist of about four red and yellow ribbons, the colour of the Spanish flag, 30 cm long. The ribbons are wound and knotted round the middle finger and dangle on the outside of the hand.

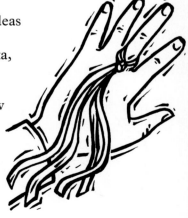

El Vito

Traditional song
English words and accompaniment by Jean Gilbert

2. Una malagueña fue
a Sevilla a ver los toros. } *repeat*
Y en la mitad del camino
se la quedaron los moros. } *repeat*

2. *A señora, 'malagueña',*
went to Seville for the bulls. } *repeat*
In the middle of the journey
she was captured by the Moors. } *repeat*

Many traditional songs from southern Spain include references to the time when
most of Spain was ruled over by the Moors.

19

Suggested accompaniment

Castanets are the traditional accompaniment to this Andalusian song. They could be played as an introduction and/or between the two verses.

Castanets

Egypt is one of the countries where castanets are known to have been used, long before the birth of Christ. They were also used by the Greeks and the Ancient Romans to accompany their ritual dances. They are found in certain areas in Italy today, although they are mainly associated with Spanish music and dancing.

Good castanets are made from very hard wood, usually granadilla or rosewood. They are made in pairs which vary slightly in pitch. The one with the higher pitch is worn on the right hand. They are usually worn dangling from the thumb and are played by curved fingers. The right hand can play a roll or 'carretilla' by making four quick strikes starting with the little finger and ending with the index finger. The left hand completes the roll making it into five beats. There are many different combinations of strikes and rolls.

The dance

This is a couple dance in flamenco style. The body is held erect with a straight back. Partners face one another to begin.

Figure 1

A music	Partners travel away from one another to the left, hands held at hip level, palms facing outwards, right hand in front. Tap left foot then
bar 1	Step left and draw right foot up to left.
bar 2	Repeat bar 1
bars 3–4	Stamp L RL R L
bars 5–8	Repeat bars 1–5 to the right with left hand in front and right hand at the back.
bars 1–8	Repeat above, to finish facing partner.
(repeat)	

(palm outwards)

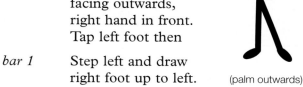

B music	Arms are now curved with right hand at hip level and left hand at head level. They change as the leading foot changes. Partners cross over and back again with the following step:
bar 9	Point right foot in front then lightly flick it back.
bar 10	Step R L R.
bar 11	Point left foot in front then lightly flick it back.
bar 12	Step LRL. Continue across then return on the repeat of the B music.

Figure 2

A music	As for the first A music, but partners go the same way.
B music	The boy kneels while the girl travels round him with the step described for the first B music.
(repeat)	Change over with the girl kneeling and the boy travelling. Just before the end the girl stands up and both dancers finish with a stamp.

Figure 3 Repeat Figure 1

Teaching the dance

Teach the steps for the A and B music separately and concentrate on them until the children are familiar with them and are enjoying the movement.

Let the children practise the stamp: R LR L R and L RL R L. Then practise the stamp at the end of two step/slides. Finally the complete step, with the arm movements, or add these later when the children begin to dance together.

Similarly with the basic step for the B music. Let the children practise without partners and the arm movements to begin with. Some children will take longer to synchronize arm and foot movements than others. Do not let this inhibit them from joining in the dancing.

Los Sanfermines

This famous fiesta takes place at the beginning of July in Pamplona. Originally a religious festival, it is also an annual excuse to revive native traditions. Fighting bulls run half a mile through narrow barricaded streets to a loading pen behind the bullfight plaza. Young men test their manhood by running with them with only a rolled-up newspaper for protection. The 'encierro' lasts only two or three minutes but it is full of danger!

The following light-hearted song is sung during the holiday.

Canción de San Fermín
Song for San Fermín

Traditional song
English words by Jean Gilbert

When sung, the words 'de enero' and 'de abril' are run together as shown by the sign ⌣ in the music. This sign is used wherever similar abbreviations are made when singing in Spanish.

Uno de enero, dos de febrero,
tres de marzo, cuatro de abril,
cinco de mayo, seis de junio,
siete de julio, San Fermín.

First of January, second of February,
third of March, fourth of April,
fifth of May, sixth of June,
seventh of July, San Fermín.

This is a useful little rhyme to help teach numbers and months of the year.
The English words of the first four lines are not intended to be sung to the tune.

Suggested accompaniment

The tunes can be played on the descant recorder. A small drum or tambour played on the beat can accompany the singing game on page 22.

Drum or tambour:

accompany the singing game on page 22.

21

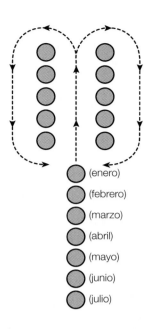

(enero)
(febrero)
(marzo)
(abril)
(mayo)
(junio)
(julio)

Singing game

Arrange the children in two lines facing one another, with seven more children at one end between the lines, representing the seven months (see diagram). As the first four lines of the song are sung, the seven children skip one at a time down through the two standing lines, each child beginning as a month is sung. At the top they skip round alternately to the left and right, and back to make one circle with the two standing lines. Sing the verse as many times as is necessary.

The next four lines, beginning 'A Pamplona', are sung as all the children skip round in their circle.

The children could choreograph a simple dance arrangement and repeat these lines as many times as required. Here are some basic patterns:

Skip round and back again.
Facing centre, skip in and out of the circle.
Skip round on the spot or with a partner.
Stand still and clap.
Dance a 'grand chain': partners face one another in the circle then skip round giving alternate hands as they pass each other to return to their own partners.

Soy de Santurce
I'm from Santurce

Traditional song
English words and accompaniment by Jean Gilbert

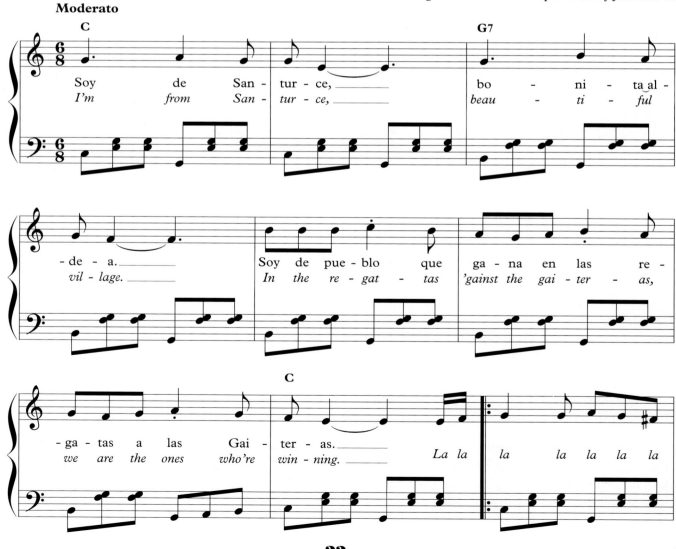

Moderato

Soy de San - tur - ce, ___ bo - ni - ta al -
I'm from San - tur - ce, ___ beau - ti - ful

-de - a. ___ Soy de pue - blo que ga - na en las re -
vil - lage. ___ In the re - gat - tas 'gainst the gai - ter - as,

-ga - tas a las Gai - ter - as. ___ La la la la la la la
we are the ones who're win - ning. ___

la   la   la   la   la   la   la   la   la   la   la,_____   la   la

la   la   la   la   la   la   la   la   la   la   la   la   la

la   la._____   Que   tu_er - es   el   mar,_____   y
For   you're_____   the   sea,_____   and

yo   soy   la_a - re - na   que   ya   no   se   mue - ve que_el
I   am   the   un - mov - ing   sand,   but   the   wa - ter   will

1.   **2.**

a - gua   la   lle - va._____   La   la   lle - va._____
ebb,   ebb   a - way._____   La   la   -way._____

Santurce is a little fishing village on the north coast of Spain where many of the festivals are connected with the sea. In the summer months and especially around 15 August, boat races and regattas as well as street music, dancing and fireworks, take place during La Semana Grande.

The 'gaiteras' are the people who play the gaita, a type of bagpipe, typical of Galicia in northern Spain. In some versions of the song the word 'traineras' (small fishing boats) is sung instead.

Movement

The lilting rhythm of this little song suggests a gentle swaying movement. Spanish children like to symbolize the sea in rows moving in alternate directions. This can be effective with large groups of children. Let them hold up models of boats or cut-out pictures on card to improvise the scene of a regatta.

For lists of other resources see page 116.

Greece

Ελλάς

FYROM*
BULGARIA
ALBANIA
TURKEY
Thrace
Macedonia
• Kastoria
GREECE
AEGEAN SEA
IONIAN SEA
TURKEY
Athens
• Olympia
Sparta •
MEDITERRANEAN
Knossos
Crete
SEA

*Former Yugoslav Republic of Macedonia

Greece is a mountainous country at the southern end of the Balkan peninsula. The Balkans are a part of south-east Europe which includes the countries of Albania, Bulgaria, Greece, Romania, part of Turkey, Bosnia-Herzegovina, Croatia, and the Federal Republic of Yugoslavia (now consisting of Serbia and Montenegro). Rugged highlands in the north of Greece form a boundary with neighbouring countries. The rest of the country is surrounded by the warm seas of the Mediterranean.

The coastline, one of the longest in Europe, is jagged, with rocky headlands, countless bays and deep inlets. There are literally hundreds of islands dotted all over the Ionian and Aegean Seas. Crete, lying to the south, is the largest of the islands.

Greece attracts a great many holiday-makers each year. They go to see wonderful ancient buildings like the temple of the Parthenon in Athens, the capital city, and the palace at Knossos on Crete, or to enjoy the beautiful islands and the hot Mediterranean climate.

For the farmers, life can be hard because the soil is generally poor and there is a water shortage in summer. Olive trees can survive in these conditions and are very important to the Greeks. Most olives are crushed to make olive oil, an important ingredient in Greek cooking. Some are picked when green, others when ripe and black. The Greeks eat them in salads or as a mid-morning snack with bread and some 'feta' cheese (made from sheep or goat's milk).

Grapes flourish in the hot, dry climate. They are grown for wine-making, for eating or for drying as currants, raisins and sultanas. Both wine and fruit are exported world wide.

History

The history of Greece stretches back over four thousand years. As early as 3000 BC, copper and tin were being mined and crafted. Great palaces like the one at Knossos were built by the Minoans (2500–1500 BC), but the Mycenaeans (1500–900 BC) were the creators of one of the greatest civilizations of all time. They built the high walls of the Acropolis in Athens and their powerful navy dominated the seas around.

The period known as the Classical Age (500-300 BC approx.) was very important. By then a common alphabet had been developed and Greece became famous for its great scientists, mathematicians, writers and philosophers.

During this great age the Greeks were fighting among themselves. Philip II of Macedonia succeeded in uniting them in 338 BC and his son Alexander the Great went on to build a great empire. After Alexander's death Greece was again invaded. It became a Roman province in 146 BC and eventually part of the eastern Roman Byzantine Empire. In AD 1453 it was overrun yet again, this time by the Turks. For 400 years Greece was part of the Turkish Ottoman Empire.

In 1821 the Greeks revolted against the Turks and, at the end of a bitter war, regained their independence in 1827. Greek Independence Day is celebrated every year on 25 March, which is a national holiday.

During the twentieth century Greece suffered during both World Wars, and a civil war from 1946–9. Greece became a republic in 1974.

The Parthenon

Language 🗜

Greek is the only language in its branch of the Indo-European family. The Greek alphabet, modelled originally on the Phoenician alphabet, became in turn the basis of the ancient Roman alphabet, and ultimately all western alphabets.

The modern Greek alphabet

Letter	Name	English equivalent
A α	alpha	A a as in 'father' (semi-long)
B β	vita	V v as in 'vine'
Γ γ	gamma	G g or Y y
Δ δ	delta	D d (soft) as 'th' in 'this'
E ε	epsilon	E e as in 'met'
Z ζ	zita	Z z
H η	ita	I i as in 'ski'
Θ θ	thita	Th th as in think
I ι	iota	I i as in 'ski'
K κ	kappa	K k
Λ λ	lamda	L l
M μ	mi	M m
N ν	ni	N n
Ξ ξ	xi	X x as in 'axe'
O o	omicron	O o as in 'dog'
Π π	pi	P p
P ρ	rho	R r (slightly rolled)
Σ σ (ς)	sigma	S s
T τ	taf	T t
Y υ	ipsilon	I i as in 'ski'
Φ φ	phi	F f
X χ	hi	H h, guttural as in 'loch'
Ψ ψ	psi	Ps ps as in 'lapse'
Ω ω	omega	O o as in 'dog'

English	Greek
one	ena
two	dio
three	tria
four	tessera
five	pente
six	exi
seven	epta
eight	okto
nine	enia
ten	deka
good morning	kalimera
good day	
good evening	kalispera
hello	yassu (familiar form)
	yassas (polite and plural form)
how are you doing?	ti kanis?
fine	kala
thank you	efharisto
please	parakalo
yes	ne
no	ohi
goodbye	adio

Many terms to do with the arts, sciences, politics and religion are from the Greek. Here are a few:

Philosophy, mathematics, physics, geometry, democracy . . .

Theatre, scene, orchestra, chorus, tragedy, comedy . . .

Music, poetry, harmony, rhythm, lyric . . .

Athlete, discus, stadium, decathlon, marathon . . .

Perhaps some children could add to this list.

Suggestions for further language activities can be found on page 7.

Food and drink

Most families eat small meals during the day. Breakfast is usually coffee and bread with honey or jam. Lunch, around 2 pm, may consist of a vegetable dish or salad, followed by a rest or 'siesta'. Shops and offices are shut until 5.30 pm.

The evening meal, however, is substantial. It is eaten late, after the heat of the day at about 8 or 9 pm, and can last for a long time. It might begin with soup or appetisers such as 'tzatziki' (cucumber and yoghurt salad) or 'taramosalata'. This is a delicious dip, originally made from 'tarama', the roe of the grey mullet. There are many popular main dishes. 'Moussaka' and

---

Horiatiki salata (Village salad)

Salads are great favourites and can be made with virtually any combination of raw vegetables with a simple dressing of olive oil and lemon or vinegar. The following recipe is very popular:

3 large beefsteak tomatoes, thinly sliced

1 medium onion, thinly sliced

100g feta cheese

1 tablespoon chopped fresh oregano

3 tablespoons olive oil

a little lemon juice or wine vinegar

freshly ground black pepper

black olives

a little garlic

Rub the inside of a salad bowl thoroughly with the garlic, then discard it.

Put in the sliced onion and tomatoes.

Crumble the feta cheese and sprinkle on top with the oregano, olives and pepper.

Mix the oil with the lemon juice or vinegar and carefully spoon it evenly over the top.

Cover and leave to stand at room temperature for about 20 minutes to allow the flavours to mingle.

Tsourekakia (Easter buns)

1 tablespoon aniseed	$\frac{1}{2}$ teaspoon salt
a little water	3–4 eggs
$1\frac{1}{2}$ tablespoons yeast	175g melted butter
150ml warm milk	225g caster sugar
$\frac{1}{2}$ tablespoon grated orange rind	1 egg yolk
675g flour	75g blanched almonds

Simmer the aniseed in a little water for 5 minutes. Strain and put aside 4 tablespoons of the liquid.

Put the yeast in a basin and mash with a little of the lukewarm milk.

Add 75g flour and mix to a batter. Cover with a cloth and put in a warm place to prove.

Sift the rest of the flour in a mixing bowl. Add the salt and orange rind.

Make a well and add the eggs, melted butter, sugar, yeast and aniseed water.

Mix well and work to a soft dough.

Cover with a cloth and leave in a warm place until the dough has doubled in size.

Turn out onto a floured board, knead lightly and break off even-sized pieces. Roll these into long 'sausages'.

Plait three of these to form the buns.

Arrange on a greased baking tray and put in a warm place to rise for the third time.

Glaze the buns with beaten egg yolk, sprinkle with chopped almonds and bake in a moderately hot oven for 30 minutes.

This quantity makes about 12 large buns but more 'mini-sized' ones could be made by reducing the size of the 'sausages' and the cooking time. They are best eaten fresh but are still delicious after a few days when toasted.

'pastitzio' are mixtures of meat and vegetables served as a casserole. 'Dolmades' are rolled vine leaves stuffed with rice and minced meat. The Greeks also enjoy seafood: octopus, squid, lobster, shrimp and mullet are frequently on the menu.

Fresh fruit will usually follow, but on special occasions there will be desserts that are traditionally very sweet. 'Baklava' and 'kataifi' are made with pastry and honey. Yoghurt and custard are also popular. There is always a good wine to go with the meal and coffee to finish. This is exceedingly strong and sweet and usually served with a glass of iced water.

Music and dancing will often accompany dinner in Greek tavernas where there are bouzouki bands and singers. The bouzouki is a traditional stringed instrument similar to a mandolin.

There are good Greek food shops in many localities nowadays. If you are lucky enough to have one around the corner, arrange some visits to explore the range of Greek foods available. Ask the children for ideas for a special Greek (cold) buffet and involve some parents, especially if they are Greek, to help arrange it. Invite some special visitors, perhaps some teachers, other parents or the shopkeeper!

Art and craft

The ancient art of pottery was practised by many early civilizations. Settlements tended to be built near rivers and lakes where clay was to be found and no doubt its use for making containers such as cooking pots and storage jars was soon discovered. There are many examples of fine Greek pottery decorated with geometric designs and figures that tell us a lot about the life of ancient Greece.

Here are some pottery ideas for the children to try. Use red clay, and provide a board for working on and a damp sponge. You will also need wooden tools, a knife and a nylon scourer for making designs and finishing off. Most clay needs to be fired or baked in a kiln to be made into a permanent substance but reinforced modelling clay will harden on its own. Glazing is applied to give a final finish and to make the clay waterproof. A detailed approach to working with clay can be found in *Clay* by Jeannie Hull (Franklin Watts, 1989).

Thumb pots

These were probably the first kind of pots ever made and are very simple for beginners.

Pat a small piece of clay into a round shape, then start making a hole in the centre with one thumb, holding the clay in the other 'cupped' hand. Fashion the pot by pinching and turning until the walls are of an even thickness. Dampen the clay with the sponge if there are any signs of cracking or splitting. To make a flat base, tap or press carefully on the board. Decorate the pot with a favourite design and leave to dry. It is a good idea to try out a few designs beforehand on a flattened piece of clay. When dry, carefully smooth or scrape any sharp edges.

Coil pots

It is easier to make larger pots by coiling, which just means building up the pot from rolled coils of clay. The art of rolling may need a little practice first!

The base is made first by rolling a coil into a spiral, then gently smoothing it over on both sides. The pot can then be built up gradually into the desired shape and finally decorated.

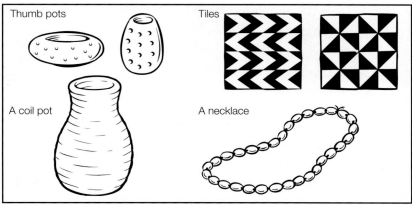

Ancient Greece

Philosophy

Socrates discussed his ideas about democratic government with his fellow Athenians in informal meetings.

Plato recorded the discussions in his book *The Republic*. **Aristotle** influenced philosophy and science long after his death in 322 BC.

Science

Eratosthenes discovered that the world was round rather than flat.

Euclid's geometry is still used today. It includes the famous theorem of **Pythagoras**.

Archimedes invented the Archimedean Screw for raising water.

Hero invented a primitive steam engine.

Hippocrates, the 'Father of Medicine', was both physician and surgeon. Today, doctors still take the 'Hippocratic Oath'.

Literature

Homer was Greece's greatest poet; it is thought that he was the author of *The Iliad* and *The Odyssey*, two epic sagas telling of the Trojan Wars and the wanderings of Odysseus.

Aeschylus, **Sophocles** and **Euripides** wrote tragic plays based on Greek legends.

Sport

The original Olympic Games were held at Olympia, in Southern Greece, every four years from 776 BC to AD 393. Sport and physical fitness were an important part of Greek life. The Marathon race commemorates a Greek  messenger who ran from Marathon to Athens (26 miles) with the news of a Greek victory over the Persian army. He then collapsed and died. The first modern Olympic Games were held in Athens in 1896.

Greece today

Main crops:
fruit, vegetables, cereals, tobacco

Main industries:
food products, metals, metal products, textiles

People's jobs:

Agricultural	21%
Industrial	28%
Other	51%

Tiles

Roll out a largish piece of clay, decorate and cut into a tile shape.

Necklaces

Make small beads or pendants and thread onto thin wire, string or strong cotton.

Decorations

Many Greek vases have geometric designs around the rims and bases and figures on the body of the vases. Some children might be experienced enough to tackle this form of decoration. Alternatively, vases and tiles could have painted decorations. Black on red or similar coloured clay works well.

Suggestions for general classroom activities can be found on page 6.

Folk costume

There is a great variety of different styles and designs among the costumes. Many reflect ancient Greek and Byzantine traditions and the kind of region in which the costumes are worn.

One of the most beautiful of women's costumes is the 'Amalia', worn originally by Queen Amalia for whom it was created and from whom the dress gets its name. The full ankle-length skirt can be any colour or variety of colours, preferably in pastel shades. It is worn with a heavily embroidered jacket and blouse with flared sleeves and long cuffs. The small red cap has a long and heavy silk tassel.

The 'foustanella' costume is worn notably by the Evzones, the Greek guards. It consists of a full-sleeved white shirt, worn under an embroidered bolero, long white woollen stockings, shoes with huge black pompoms on upturned toes and a full pleated white skirt, the 'foustanella' (See centre colour section).

Festivals

There are two main secular festivals celebrated in Greece today. Independence Day ('Epanastassi tou 1821') on 25 March is both a national and religious holiday. Parades and dancing are held to celebrate the beginning of the revolt against Turkish rule in 1821, whilst church services honour the news given to Mary that she was to become the Mother of Christ. 28 October, known as Ohi Day ('Imera tou Ohi'), commemorates Metaxas's one-word reply to Italy's 1940 invasion ultimatum: 'Ohi!' (No!), with parades, folk dancing and feasting.

May Day ('Protomaya') has become a great urban holiday when townspeople traditionally make for the countryside to return with bunches of wild flowers. Wreaths are hung on doorways or balconies until they are burnt on Midsummer Eve. There are many local and regional festivals including numerous saints' days as well as fishing and wine festivals. Celebrations usually take place on the eve of the festival, the 'paramoni', and each province will have its own local dance with regional characteristics.

The lively dance 'Kastorianos' comes from the town of Kastoria in the geographical region of Macedonia, in the north. According to legend, the town was founded by Orestes.

Gathering olives

Chariot racing

Relaxing to music

Kastorianos

Traditional dance from the town of Kastoria, Macedonia
Accompaniment by Jean Gilbert

Suggested accompaniment

Drum or tambour.

The dance

Dancers stand by a partner and form a circle, holding hands.

bars 1–8   8 double steps starting with the right foot, travelling to the right, always in the same direction.

bars 9–12   2 sets of scissor steps, facing centre.

bars 13–20   Drop hands and face partners. Place right foot in front on heel, then beat 4 times with the left fist on to the right palm (2 bars). Step back onto right foot. Repeat to the left (2 bars).

Repeat both sides.
The dance continues.

Steps

Double steps   In circle formation, turn the body to the right. Step right, bring left foot up to right heel, step right again and pause (1 bar). Continue with the left foot, going round in the circle anti-clockwise.

Scissor steps   Facing the centre, step right, cross left foot in front of right and step, keeping weight on right foot, then step onto right foot again and pause (1 bar). Repeat to the left to complete a set of scissor steps (2 bars altogether).

Throughout the dance the head and shoulders lean towards the leading foot. There is a strong focus on the beat. It will be helpful to listen to the music first and clap the beat.

Makedonia xakusti
Famous Macedonia

Traditional song
English words and accompaniment by Jean Gilbert

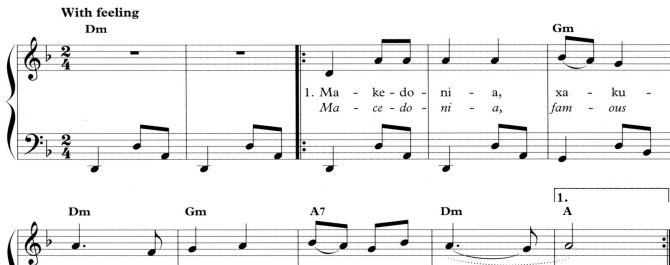

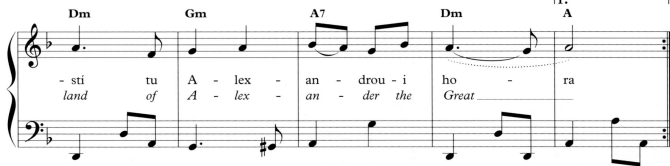

Sing this fine song firmly and with conviction. The melody of the first section, notes D F G A B♭, could be played on descant recorders as an introduction.

Let the children listen to the recording and see if they can hear the bouzouki in the accompaniment. It is a common Greek folk instrument, rather like a mandolin or lute.

2. Ise ke tha'se Elliniki
Ellinon to kamari.
K'emis ta Ellinopula
su plekume stefani.

2. You were Greek and ever will be,
the pride of all the Greek people.
And we the young Greek children too,
we are plaiting a wreath for you.

A bouzouki player

1. Μακεδονία ξακουστή
του Αλεξάνδρου η χώρα.
που έδιωξε τους βάρβαρους
κ'ελεύθερ' είσαι τώρα.

2. Είσαι και θά' σαι Ελληνική
Ελλήνων το καμάρι.
Κ'εμείς τα Ελληνόπουλα
σου πλέκουμε στεφάνι.

Lènim 'thi Mais

Helen, May has come

Traditional song from Thrace
Accompaniment by Jean Gilbert

Vivace ♩ = 132

INTRODUCTION

Dance

Lè - nim 'thi Ma - is ki'a - man jiel' - a - man,

Lè - nim 'thi Ma - is ki a - ni - xi.

These English words are not intended to be sung, for there can be no substitute for the sound of the Greek in this joyful spring song.

Helen, May has come, tra la la la la
Helen, May has come and spring is here,
May has come and spring is here,
And summer has arrived.

'Lènim 'thi Mais' is presented here as a dance, although the recording includes verses of the song. These enhance the appeal of the dance music and, for those children who would like to sing as well, the first verse is given.

The dance comes from Thrace, the most easterly province of mainland Greece, and is traditionally danced in May to celebrate the coming of spring. The line of dancers dances through every building and house, as well as open spaces, with more and more people joining in all the time.

Dancers join hands in an open circle which later develops into a chain. Turn right to face the line of dance.

bar 1   Double step starting with the right foot and moving to the right.

bar 2   Double step with the left foot, continuing to the right.

bar 3   With back to the line of dance, double step (RLR) on the spot, raising arms, elbows bent.

bar 4   Facing the line of dance, double step (LRL) on the spot, lowering arms.

This sequence of steps is repeated as the leader takes the line of dancers into many kinds of shapes.

Double step is described on page 32.

Tha páro miá psarovarka

I'll take a fishing boat

Traditional song, words translated by Sofia Charalambous
English words and accompaniment by Jean Gilbert

This simple little song is typical of many island songs. It is a great favourite at festival times.

Greek dance from the Islands
Adapted by Jean Gilbert

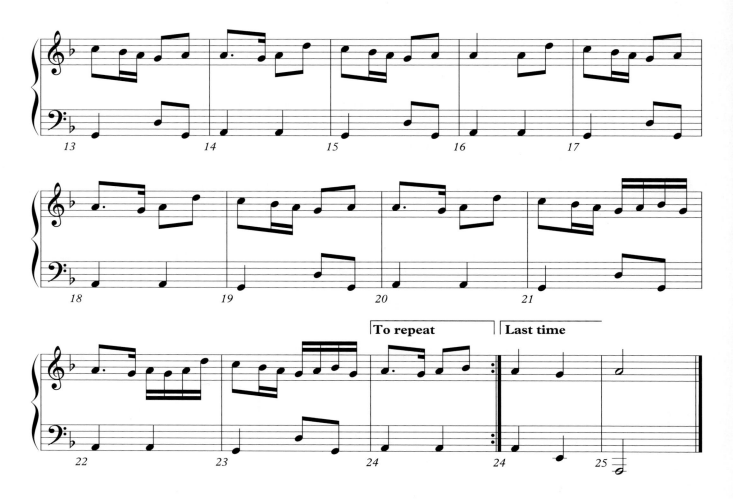

To repeat | Last time

The simplicity of this dance is typical of many that are danced at festival times when everyone likes to join in.

The dance is performed in a semicircle. Hands are lightly linked and arms move backwards and forwards with the movement.

bar 1   Step forward with the right foot moving arms forward and up. Bring left foot forward and step left, right.

bar 2   Step back with left foot moving arms down. Bring right foot back and step right, left.

The dance continues with this very simple movement.

A slight variation can be introduced halfway through the music at the end of bar 12:

bar 12   Hop on the left foot to

bar 13   step forward with right foot. Bring left foot forward and step left, right. Hop on the right foot to

bar 14   step back with the left foot. Bring right foot back and step right, left. The movement of the arms continues as before.

Suggested accompaniment

Drum or tambour

For lists of other resources see page 117.

Bulgaria

България

ROMANIA

R. Danube

F. R. YUGOSLAVIA (Serbia)

BULGARIA

Balkan Range

Valley of the Roses

•Sofia

•Karlova
Sredna Gora
Mountains

BLACK
SEA

•Kyustendil

R. Struma

R. Maritsa

Plain of Thrace

FYROM*

TURKEY

GREECE

*Former Yugoslav Republic of Macedonia

Bulgaria, in south-east Europe, is a small, mountainous country on the eastern side of the Balkan Peninsula.

It has some of the finest scenery in Europe, with forests of oak, beech and fir trees covering over a quarter of the land. Farmers allow their sheep to spend the summer in the mountains, and then to come down for the winter. Herds of horses and cattle roam the lower mountain slopes. Wheat, maize and sunflowers grow in the open fields and there are vineyards where excellent grapes are grown. The wine from these grapes is an important export.

Sofia, the capital city, lies on a high open plateau near the main pass leading to the western border with former Yugoslavia. Here, in the interior of the country, the summers are hot and dry but the winters are bitterly cold. Winter visitors go to ski on the snow-covered mountain slopes. In the summer the great attraction is the beautiful coast of the Black Sea with its sandy beaches and sunny warm weather.

Between the Balkan and the Sredna Gora mountain ranges is the sight for which Bulgaria is celebrated, the Valley of Roses. Here there are vast stretches of rose fields that produce 70% of the world's supply of attar of roses, a precious oil used for making the finest perfumes. 2,000 roses are needed for a single gram of the oil. The roses are in bloom from about the end of May, and picking begins before dawn, when the fragrance of the petals is at its height. The Festival of Roses ('Festival na Rozata') celebrated during the first half of June is a fairly recent event. Tourists come to see the rose-picking at dawn, the parade of flowers and the songs and dances that follow.

History

The Bulgarian people are of the same Slav origin as the Russian and Polish people and speak a similar language. Their ancestors settled in the Balkans during the sixth and seventh centuries AD.

At the end of the seventh century, a Turkic tribe known as the Bulgars moved westwards from central Asia and arrived in the Balkans. They eventually mixed with the Slavs but gave their name to the state which they helped found in AD 681. Bulgaria is one of the oldest surviving states in Europe.

During the ninth century the country flourished when the Bulgarian ruler Prince Boris adopted Orthodox Christianity as the official state religion. During this time, the Cyrillic alphabet (see page 41), now used by the Russians and Serbs as well, was created. It was named after one of its creators, Cyril, and every year its founding is commemorated on 24 May, the Day of Bulgarian Education and Culture ('Kiril i Metodi') which is a public holiday.

Bulgaria was later ruled over for five centuries by the Ottoman Turks until liberation by the Russians led to independence once again in 1878. Liberation Day on 3 March is one of Bulgaria's major national holidays.

Bulgaria is now a republic. The population is mostly Slavonic but also includes Turkish, Jewish, Armenian, Greek and gypsy minorities.

Some famous people and events

St Cyril (827–69) and his brother **St Methodius** (826–85) were known as 'the Apostles of the Slavs'. They invented a script called the 'Cyrillic alphabet' and prepared a Slav translation of the Scriptures.

Vasil Levski (1837–73) was one of the principal leaders of a nationwide rising against Turkish rule. He was eventually caught and executed, but his life has become legendary and he is still regarded in Bulgaria as a great national hero.

The Four Gospels were written and illuminated in 1355–6 for Tsar Ivan Alexander. During the Turkish occupation, the book was taken out of Bulgaria. It was discovered in a Greek monastery in 1837 by an English traveller, Robert Curzon. It was bequeathed to the British Museum in 1917 and is now in the British Library. It is known as the **Curzon Bible** and is the most celebrated example of Bulgarian medieval art.

Boris Christoff (1914–93) was one of the greatest bass-baritones of his time. His most famous role was Boris Godunov in the opera of that name by Mussorsky.

Main crops:

wheat, maize, barley, sugar beet, grapes, tobacco

Main industries:

textiles, food, beverages, tobacco products

People's jobs:

Agricultural	11%
Industrial	37%
Other	52%

Language 🪩

Bulgarian is a Slav language belonging to the same group as Russian and Serbo-Croat. The Cyrillic alphabet is shared by all three languages with a few minor differences:

Cyrillic alphabet	English equivalent
А а	A a as in 'father'
Б б	B b
В в	V v
Г г	G g as in get
Д д	D d
Е е	E e as in 'engine'
Ж ж	Zh zh as in 'measure'
З з	Z z as in 'zebra'
И и	I i pronounced 'ee' as in 'sheep'
Й й	Y y as in 'yes'
К к	K k
Л л	L l
М м	M m
Н н	N n
О о	O o as in 'hot'
П п	P p
Р р	R r
С с	S s as in 'soft'
Т т	T t
У у	U u as in 'rule'
Ф ф	F f
Х х	H h as in 'loch'
Ц ц	Ts ts as in 'cats'
Ч ч	Ch ch as in 'church'
Ш ш	Sh sh as in 'ship'
Щ щ	Sht sht as in 'sloshed'
Ъ ъ	U u as in 'squirrel'
Ь ь	Y y as in 'yodel'
Ю ю	Yu yu as in 'you'
Я я	Ya ya as in 'yarn'

English	Bulgarian
one	ednó
two	dve
three	tri
four	chétiri
five	pet
six	shest
seven	sédem
eight	ossem
nine	dévet
ten	désset

English	Bulgarian
good morning	dobró útro
good afternoon	dóbar den
good evening	dóbar vécher
hello!	zdravéy! (s) zdravéyte! (pl)
how are things?	kak si? (s) kak ste? (pl)
fine	dobré
thank you	blagodaryá
please	mólya
yes	da (a horizontal shake of the head means 'yes')
no	ne (a nod means 'no')
goodbye	dovízhdane

Suggestions for language activities can be found on page 7.

Food and drink

A ceremonial loaf for Easter

The Bulgarians have borrowed many good things from others so that dishes popular in Bulgaria may be similar to those in Greece and Turkey.

Yoghurt (a Turkish word) is very important to the Bulgarians who call it 'kiselo mlyako', meaning sour milk. The milk is soured by an organism called 'bacillus Bulgaricus'. The best Bulgarian yoghurt is made from sheep's milk and is always eaten very fresh. The average Bulgarian family gets through several pints a day, though it is usually cow's yoghurt in the cities.

Special national dishes include Shópska salad and 'taratór', a cold soup which is perfect for hot summer days. There are recipes for both these dishes on page 42. Other traditional dishes are white sheep's cheese baked with eggs, 'kebapcheta' (minced meat rolled into sausage shapes and grilled), 'shish kebab' and 'moussaka'.

There is good Bulgarian wine to go with the meal. Coffee invariably comes in the form of strong, sweet espresso or 'tursko' (Turkish coffee) and is often drunk with a glass of cold juice.

Shópska Saláta (Salad Sofia-style)

Mix together equal quantities of chopped (diced) cucumber, tomatoes, peppers, plus some raw onion, and, if popular, a little chopped hot green chilli. Pile on a plate and cover with grated feta cheese (called 'síréné' in Bulgarian). The proportions and even the ingredients may be varied according to taste and availability. Cucumber alone is very good with grated feta.

Note Peasants from the Sofia district are known as 'shopi'.

Taratór (Cold yoghurt and cucumber soup)

500g (2 cups) plain yoghurt
300g cucumber, peeled and finely chopped
6–8 cloves of garlic crushed or finely chopped

1 dessertspoon olive oil
10–12 walnut kernels, chopped or crushed
2 cups cold water

Stir the yoghurt well.

Add the cucumber, walnuts, garlic, olive oil, salt to taste and water.

Stir well. Sprinkle with chopped fresh fennel before serving.

The proportions of the ingredients may be altered according to taste. Some Bulgarians prefer to add very little water so that the soup is more creamy.

Biskviti sus síréné (Feta biscuits with caraway seeds)

250g margarine
300g plain flour (white or brown)

300g feta cheese
Caraway seeds

Mix the margarine and flour.

Crumble the feta cheese and add to the mixture.

Roll onto a floured board and make into biscuits about $\frac{1}{2}$ cm thick.

Sprinkle with caraway seeds and bake on a greased tray in a moderate oven until cooked (about 20 or more minutes, according to thickness). They should look pinkish brown when ready.

Makes about 30 round biscuits 6cm across.

The above recipes could form the basis of a light Bulgarian-style meal.

Art and craft

Many of the local handcrafts have a strong Turkish–Oriental influence. Bulgarian craftworkers are noted for their rugs and delicate metalwork.

Martenítsa

The children could make a 'martenítsa', with little red and white tassels, and learn about a very old Bulgarian spring custom, the giving of martenítsas on 1 March. These are presented to relatives and friends to offer congratulations on the approaching spring and to wish them health and happiness in the months ahead. Whoever gives them says 'Chestita Baba Marta', which means 'Happy Grandmother March'. Traditionally, martenítsas are given not only to people, but also to domestic animals, fruit trees, vines and even tools, looms, etc. They are worn until the first stork or swallow is seen; then they are hung on a bush or put under a stone, preferably near a stork's nest. Red is held to be a magical colour which protects from sickness and other evils, and red and white is considered to be a lucky combination. Traditionally the martenítsa was tied around the wrist of the recipient but nowadays it is usually tied in a bow and pinned to the lapel.

A martenítsa consists of two woollen threads, one red and one white, twisted together. It may also have all kinds of additional ornaments such as tassels or bobbles at each end. Tassels may be tied to represent human figures. These are made by taking about 20 lengths of about 10 cm long, doubling them over and tying them.

Surváchkas

At New Year ('Súrva'), children make 'surváchkas'. With these they tap people on the back and recite:

> Súrva, súrva year!
> Merry year!
> Full ears in the fields,
> yellow corn-cobs on the fence,
> red grapes on the vine,
> and yellow quinces in the garden.
> A house full of silk,
> a purse full of money ...
> Súrva, súrva year,
> till next year with health,
> till next year, till Amen.

The children are usually given sweets or coins in return.

A surváchka is made of a small flexible branch of a fruit-bearing tree such as hazel, mulberry, plum or pear. In Bulgaria the favourite tree for this purpose is the cornel-cherry which is especially suitable because its twigs and branches sprout in pairs, not alternately. It also flowers early and has buds that can be put in pastries, etc. in much the same way as charms are put in Christmas puddings. When cornel-cherry is used, the twigs are tied to form circles and the whole wand is decorated with things symbolizing good luck and abundance, such as strings of popcorn, dried prunes and other fruit, beans, nuts, small onions, garlic cloves, small rings of bread, wool and ribbons, preferably red.

Suggestions for general classroom activities can be found on page 6.

Folk costume

All Bulgarian folk costumes convey information about the wearer, such as from which region or even village a person comes; what a man's profession is; whether a girl is unattached or betrothed; whether a woman is a newly-married bride, the mother of a family or a widow; and what activity or ritual a person is currently performing.

The most ancient item common to all Bulgarian folk costumes is the shirt or chemise, known as the 'riza' or 'koshoulya'. It is made from a single length of white hemp, linen or cotton cloth, folded at the shoulders and slashed at the neck to admit the head with sleeves sewn in at right angles to the body and various gores and gussets to provide extra width. The cut is basically the same for both sexes but, while the woman's riza is mid-calf or ankle-length, that of the man is knee-length and may be worn inside or outside various types of trousers. Bulgarian costumes are classified according to what is worn with the basic riza.

Sofia region: woman's costume

White chemise embroidered in red on hem, sleeves and neck opening.

'Sukman' (overdress) in black or dark blue wool, decorated with spiral ornamentation in white braid.

Hide sandals

Special features added for Lazaruvané

White and red apron trimmed with lace.

In most Bulgarian women's costumes an apron is obligatory. The Sofia costume is an exception and the apron is added for special occasions such as Lazaruvané.

Head-dress of flowers (artificial), pampas-type grass, beads and coins.

A kerchief for waving is a usual addition, as shown in the illustration in the colour section.

Sofia region: man's costume

White shirt embroidered with white, red and blue thread.

White trousers decorated in white at the knee and pockets.

Black jacket decorated with red and white braid.

Wide cummerbund or sash of tartan-type weave (black, grey and red) wrapped several times round waist.

Black sheepskin hat.

Hide sandals.

Festivals

Many of the old customs and folklore still survive in country areas, though in most of the cities they have fallen into disuse as a result of industrialization.

Different seasons have their special festivals and customs. On New Year's Day, children wander around carrying a stick or surváchka (see page 43). They tap people on the back to bring them good luck. Another very popular token of good luck is the gift of the martenítsa on 1 March to signify the coming of spring (see page 42). The custom known as Lazaruvané described below marks the arrival of spring itself. Decorating Easter eggs is a custom found in many countries in Eastern Europe. In Bulgaria they are tucked into a round ceremonial loaf to form a design.

Other customs are connected with the protection of people and crops. Masked dancers clothed in goat skins and bells dance round villages to bring fertility and health, while special herbs can ward off unseen evils. The ritual pruning of the vines that takes place on St Trifan's Day, 14 February, is one of many customs that can be traced back to the ancient Thracians.

Lazaruvané

The following songs are all connected with the Bulgarian spring folk custom called Lazaruvané which is performed on St Lazarus's Day (Lazarovden), the day before Palm Sunday. On this day, young girls not yet old enough to marry dress up in their best national costumes and go round their village singing and dancing in order to bring health, happiness and prosperity to its inhabitants. The repertoire connected with this custom is very large since the young girls, the 'lázarki', sing songs appropriate to the place or person addressed. Unfortunately, like many other customs, Lazaruvané has largely fallen into disuse as a result of industrialization, but it is still performed at events such as folk festivals and school concerts.

Most of the songs in this section are in dialect with departures from standard Bulgarian.

Local singers often sing in a special way, referred to in the West as 'open throated'. The throat is not, in fact 'open', but extremely constricted. This produces a rich and powerful sound which can vary from district to district.

Kadé nié pominolé
Where we pass

Traditional song

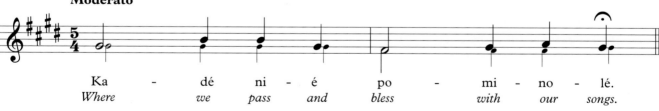

Kadé nié pominalé
rodilo sé, prerodilo.
Ta na zemnya nategnalo,
ot dva klasa – shinik zhito,
ot dvé gizhi – chebar vino.

Where we pass and bless with our songs,
There the earth brings forth bumper crops.
Heavily they weigh on the earth,
From just two ears – one sack of grain,
From just two grapes – one cask of wine.

This song is from the Kyustendíl area, famous for its apple and cherry orchards. Here village houses may be scattered over a wide area, and this song is sung as the lázarki walk through the fields to visit more distant homes. Each line is sung to the tune shown above, and the simple melody could be played on the descant recorder and embroidered by adding a second part as indicated.

Ovcharova malé
Shepherd's mother

Traditional song

Ov	- cha	- ro	- va	ma	- lé,___	ov	- cha	- ro	- va	ma	- lé!
Shep	*- herd's*	*mo*	*- ther,*	*hey*	*there,* ___	*shep*	*- herd's*	*mo*	*- ther,*	*hey*	*there!*

Ovcharova malé,
ya izlez navǔnka.
Pogleday nagoré,
pogleday nadolu,
polé sé beleyé
sǔs beli agǔntsa.
Gora sé cherneyé
sǔs cherni erentsa.

Shepherd's mother, hey there!
Leave your house, come outside!
Take a look up yonder,
take a look down yonder!
See, the plain's all white now,
white with little lambkins!
See, the wood's all black now,
black with kids and goat flocks!

Each line is repeated and sung to the melody above.

The melody could be played by descant recorders as an introduction and the lines sung by small groups or individual children.

This song comes from a village near Karlovo in the Rose Valley, which is famous for its oil-bearing roses. Although the song calls on the shepherd's mother to come and see the enormous number of lambs and kids which her son has raised, the song is actually sung to a shepherd.

Chelitsé medna
Honey bee

Traditional song

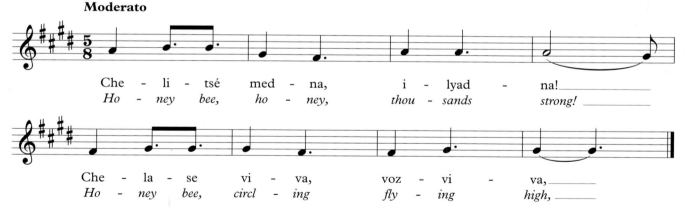

Chelitsé medna, ilyadna!
Chela se viva, vozviva,
okolo krusha kitusha,
ta i tsvetetsa bereshé,
da pravi gǔsti medové'
da pravi gǔsti medové.

Honey bee, honey, thousands strong!
Honey bee circling, flying high,
all round the pear tree in full bloom,
harvesting, gath'ring from its flowers,
honey, thick honey you will make,
honey, thick honey you will make.

This song is from Sofia, the capital. As its title suggests, it is sung in front of beehives. Many Bulgarian customs involve animals such as sheep, cows and horses, reflecting the time when they represented the main source of prosperity. Each group of two lines is sung to the melody shown.

Pravo trakijsko horo

Traditional dance from Thrace
Music adapted by Jean Gilbert

Presto ♩. = 144

Repeat details: Intro x2, A x2, B x4, A x2, B x4, C x4, D x4

INTRODUCTION

poco a poco accel. al fine

This dance from Thrace is known as a 'horo'. It is danced in an open circle or chain, a form typical of many dances from this region.

The following series of steps can be danced to the music of this horo. Because they are simple and would be well-known to most Bulgarians, they are often introduced to start off the dancing and to encourage everyone to join in.

Hands are joined and held at shoulder level in the 'W' position. Knees are kept relaxed and the back straight. The movement forms a zig-zag in and out of the circle.

Starting with the right foot, go forward, diagonally to the right, with small steps:

bar 1   right, left (quick-quick)

bar 2   right (slow)

bar 3   left (slow)

then back, diagonally to the right, with the same steps.

The following variation can be introduced to the steps going diagonally forward: RL (RLR) (LRL) – with three quick steps in the time of one slow one – to the same rhythm of 'quick-quick, slow, slow'. The same steps as before are used to dance back: RL R L.

The dance

Introduction	form a line or open circle and join hands with a 'W' hold at shoulder level.
A music	8 zig-zags with steps described above.
B music	8 zig-zags with the variation going forward.
A music	as before.
B music	as before.
C music	as for A music.
D music	as for B music.

Kralyo portalyo

Traditional children's game
Translated by Eleana Haworth

Kra - lyo por - ta - lyo, kra - lyo por - ta - lyo. Ya - bal - ka i - li kru - sha?

The following children's game is very similar to our own 'Oranges and Lemons'. Although it does not relate to any specific festival, it is popular during such holiday times. The words 'kralyo portalyo' have no special meaning, but a literal translation would be 'O King Portal (gate)'. The Bulgarian words have been kept in the English version.

Kralyo portalyo, kralyo portalyo,
otvori porti, kralyo portalyo,
che shte zamine, kralyo portalyo,
tzaryova voyska, kralyo portalyo.

Question: Yabalka ili krusha?

Kralyo portalyo, kralyo portalyo,
open the big gates, kralyo portalyo,
for the King's army, kralyo portalyo,
is now departing, kralyo portalyo.

Question: *Apple or pear?*

The game

Two children hold hands, raising their arms high, forming an arch under which the other children pass, again holding hands. Everyone sings the song. At the end, the last child passing through the arch is stopped as the two 'arch' children lower their arms to 'catch' him/her. The captive is asked to choose 'apple' or 'pear'. Depending on the answer, the child stands either on the left or the right hand side, and as the song is sung again and again two teams are formed. When all the children have joined one of the teams, they play tug-of-war. Whichever team manages to pull the other across a line drawn on the ground is the winner.

Кральо портальо, кральо портальо,

отвори порти, кральо портальо,

че ще замине, кральо портальо,

царьова войска, кральо портальо.

Въпрос: Ябълка или круша?

The words in Bulgarian

For lists of other resources see page 117.

Spain

Costumes from Murcia

Greece

The foustanella and Amalia costumes

Bulgaria

Costumes from the Sofia region

Hungary

Costumes from central Hungary

Czech Republic

Costumes from Bohemia

Germany

Costumes from Bavaria

France

Costumes from Brittany

Sweden

Costumes from Rättvik, Dalecarlia

Hungary

Magyarország

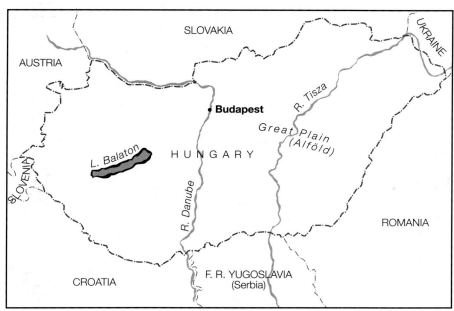

Hungary is one of the smaller countries in central Europe. It has no sea coast and no really high mountains but there are scenic rivers, rolling downlands and a vast and beautiful lake, Balaton, which has become a popular holiday resort.

The great river Danube flows through the centre of Budapest, the capital. It divides the two halves of the city (Buda and Pest) and also the country as it flows south. The land east of the Danube is called the Alföld. This is a vast, open plain where the soil is rich and black and the summers long, hot and dry. These are ideal conditions for growing crops. Wheat grown here produces a high quality flour dough from which very thin pastry can be made. Hungarian pastry cakes like strudels are delicious!

Splendid horses are bred in Hungary. The Hungarian light cavalry called the Hussars were famous. Their skilful horsemanship and fine uniforms were admired and copied by armies in other countries. (The word 'húsz' means 'twenty': one unit comprises twenty men or Hussars.)

History

Present-day Hungary was occupied by the Romans until they were driven out by the Huns, a fearsome, warlike tribe who came from the east beyond the Volga river. The breakup of the Hun empire was followed by further invasions.

The Hungarians call themselves 'Magyars'. This was the name of a nomadic tribe of herdsmen who had settled in the great plain of the Alföld by the end of the ninth century. The Magyars originally came from the plains, land west of the

Ural mountains. Their language, a branch of Finno–Ugric, is the language spoken in Hungary today.

Hungary became a Christian country when the Pope created the ruling prince Stephen, King of Hungary in AD 1000. King Stephen is regarded as the real founder of the Hungarian state. St Stephen's Day on 20 August is one of Hungary's biggest celebrations.

In 1541 the country became a province of the Ottoman Empire when the Turks penetrated into central Europe, and part of the Austrian Empire when they were driven out.

Hungary regained its independence after the First World War. Today it is a republic in which great social and political changes are taking place, as in other neighbouring countries.

Some famous people

Music

Hungarian music is sometimes mistakenly called 'gypsy music' as it is often played by gypsy violinists. Their music is mainly inspired by Hungarian folk melodies.

Folk music is an important feature of the work of the Hungarian composers **Béla Bartók** (1881–1945) and **Zoltán Kodály** (1882–1967). Bartók visited remote districts collecting the music of the peasants with his early recording equipment while Kodály used old tunes in his influential work in music education.

Ferencz (Franz) Liszt (1811–86) was famous as a brilliant pianist. His compositions such as the *Hungarian Rhapsodies* reflect the 'gypsy' side of his character.

Science

Dennis Gábor (1900–79) invented holography (three-dimensional photography).

Eugene Wigner (1902–95) won the Nobel Prize for his work on subatomic particles.

John von Neumann (1903–57) made important contributions to many fields of science. He was largely responsible for the theoretical design of the computer.

Film

Famous Hungarians in the field of cinema include the film-maker **Sir Alexander Korda** (Sándor Korda), the director **Michael Curtis** (Mihály Kertész) and actors **George Sanders**, **Leslie Howard** and **Zsa Zsa Gábor**.

People's jobs:

Agricultural	10%
Industrial	37%
Other	53%

Main crops:

wheat, maize, barley, sugar beet, potatoes

Main industries:

engineering, chemicals

Language

Hungarian or 'Magyar' is a unique language. It is unrelated to the Indo–European languages but belongs to the Finno–Ugric group which includes Finnish and Estonian.

English	Hungarian
one	egy
two	kettö
three	három
four	négy
five	öt
six	hat
seven	hét
eight	nyolc
nine	kilenc
ten	tíz
good morning	jó reggelt!
good day	jó napot!
good evening	jó estét!
hello	szia!
how are you?	hogy vagy?
fine	jól
thank	köszönöm
please	kérem
yes	igen
no	nem
goodbye	szia!

Suggestions for language activities can be found on page 7.

Food and drink

Like every other nation, the Hungarians love eating and drinking. Any special occasion is a time for a celebratory meal when families gather round long tables in somebody's home, a café or restaurant.

Pogácsa (Savoury scones)

The following simple recipe was given to me by József Baracsi:

100g self raising flour	25g grated cheese
25g salted margarine	1 egg, separated

Rub the margarine into the flour and add the grated cheese.

Make a 'well' and put in the beaten egg yolk.

Work the ingredients together. If necessary add some water to soften the mixture.

Roll out the dough to a thickness of about 2cm.

Cut into scone shapes, 5cm across.

Brush the top with beaten egg white.

Bake in a moderate oven, gas mark 5, 190° C (375° F) for about 25 minutes or until golden brown.

Makes about 6 scones.

Paprikás krumpli (Paprika potato)

Judith Szénàsi gave me one of her favourite recipes from Budapest.

2 red peppers, sliced
2 onions, peeled and sliced
1 garlic clove
a good dash of Hungarian paprika (to taste)
1 tablespoon vegetable oil
1 Hungarian sausage ('kolbasz') or an ordinary (ring) smoked sausage
2 large potatoes, peeled and sliced
1 tablespoon tomato purée

Braise the onions and peppers in oil with the garlic.

Add $\frac{1}{2}$ teaspoon black pepper and cook for 5–10 minutes.

Add the paprika, tomato purée and sliced sausage with $\frac{1}{2}$ cupful of water. Leave to simmer for 5 minutes.

Add the potatoes. Cook for 20 minutes on low heat.

Add some sour cream or yoghurt and serve with rice, pasta or white or wholemeal bread.

The main meal of the day is likely to be lunch. For most Hungarians this will be soup followed by a meat dish or occasionally fish and a dessert which is a kind of pastry. The meal usually finishes with strong coffee very similar to the Italian espresso.

Hungarian food is usually strongly spiced. One of the most characteristic flavours comes from the paprika plant which flourishes in the hot, dry summers of the Great Plain. Most tables carry a little dish or shaker filled with red paprika powder alongside the salt and pepper.

'Goulash' is probably one of the best-known dishes associated with Hungary. This is a substantial meat soup prepared with onions and paprika to which cubed potatoes, parsnips, carrots and celeriac are added. There are many delicious dishes based on fish that are caught in the rivers. Carp is very popular, and visitors to Lake Balaton will surely be tempted to try the fogas. This is the pike-perch, a lean fish with white meat, full of flavour. It can only be found in this lake in Hungary. There is always a fine wine, red or white, to go with the meal.

Art and craft

Make and decorate large white doilies with white paper and felt tip pens. Many beautiful flower designs can be seen on traditional Hungarian blouses. Favourite flowers are roses, carnations, forget-me-nots, and tulips with intertwining leaves. Colours used are mainly pastel: pink, red, blue, yellow and some green.

Folk costume

Nearly every village in Hungary has its own folk costumes. They are among the most beautiful in Europe and have a distinctive style. Women's costumes feature full skirts bulked out by several white starched petticoats, and colourfully embroidered blouses. For men there are two main styles. One is based on black, tight-fitting trousers tucked into black boots; the alternative costume includes the white linen divided skirt or trousers called 'gatya'. This is the one that has been illustrated in the colour section. Both costumes come from central Hungary.

The national costume is based on the colours red, white and green. This is worn for special anniversaries, festivals and national days in the towns and cities.

Here is a simple outline for children:

Girls White blouse and skirt with a green apron and red waistcoat. Headwear consists of a simple headband with red ribbons at the back.

Boys White shirt with bloused sleeves and laced cuffs. Tight black trousers, black waistcoat and black top boots.

Examples of flower patterns

A suggestion for a doily design

Suggestions for general classroom activities can be found on page 6.

Festivals

Hungary is rich in seasonal and ritual festivals. Many customs are to do with the major events of life — birth, marriage and death. Others run parallel to the seasons of the year, and there are festivals associated with saints' days, in common with other countries.

Weddings, traditionally held in the autumn after the busy summer season, are occasions for merry-making and may last for several days. Special dances include a pillow dance performed by the bridesmaids with decorated pillows (presents for the bride) and a cook's dance when cooking utensils are carried to catch coins that are thrown in. Guests may carry green branches decorated with hemp, a sign of fertility.

Easter ('húsvét') is a young people's festival. The curious custom of the sprinkling or splashing of the girls and women probably dates back to an ancient fertility ritual. The young men visit the houses of the girls with a bucket of water, nowadays perfume instead! The sprinkling of the girls is said to help them grow more beautiful. In return for their efforts the boys receive painted eggs.

May Day ('májusfaállitás') welcomes the spring, which is also a time for courting. Decorated boughs of young May trees are set up by the boys in front of the houses of the girls they would like to marry.

Whitsuntide ('pünkösd') is the time of the flowering of the peony, known as the Whitsun red rose. It is often used in the making of the crown of the Whitsun Queen, traditionally a young girl, who is taken in procession from house to house through the village.

There are two major harvest festivals. During the Feast of Wheat ('arató ünnep') in late June or July, the dough for bread is modelled into different shapes, and wreaths or 'corn babies' are presented to the farmers. The grape harvest ('szüret') takes place in September or early October. Large grape wreaths decorated with coloured ribbons and flowers are carried through the village to the village hall. Both festivals are followed by feasting and dancing.

At Christmas ('Karácsony'), nativity plays are performed by players who go from house to house carrying their home-made manger with them. After the play the performers are rewarded with some refreshments.

Szép szakmári lányok

The following dance, set to the tune of this Easter song on page 54, is for couples and is more suitable for older children. The dance steps are described on page 57. Teach each step first using the whole tune and as many repeats as necessary. Then arrange the steps to form a simple dance, getting ideas from the children. Here is one arrangement, where the tune is played three times:

Couples face one another with the girl's hands on the boy's shoulders and the boy's hands on the girl's waist.

bars 1–8	8 csárdás (chardash) steps to the (boy's) right.
bars 9–16	8 csárdás steps to the (boy's) left.
bars 1–8	8 turning rida steps to the right (twice round). Couples have the same hold but the body is slightly turned.
bars 9–16	8 turning rida steps to the left (twice round).

bars 1–8	4 foot-swinging steps. Couples dance side by side, the girl's left hand on the boy's right shoulder and the boy's right hand around the girl's waist.
bars 9–12	Couples now separate and dance on their own. 4 turning rida steps to the right.
bars 13–16	4 turning rida steps to the left.

Szép szakmári lányok

Szakmár village girls

Traditional song
English words and accompaniment by Jean Gilbert

Allegretto

(Dance speed ♩ = 116)

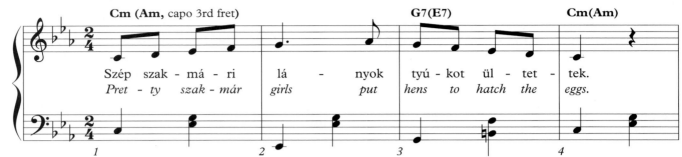

Szép szak - má - ri lá - nyok tyú - kot ül - tet - tek.
Pret - ty szak - már girls put hens to hatch the eggs.

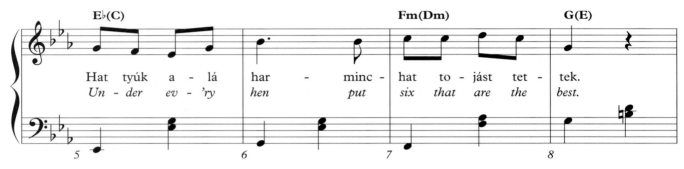

Hat tyúk a - lá har - minc - hat to - jást tet - tek.
Un - der ev - 'ry hen put six that are the best.

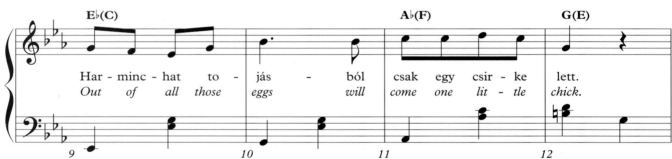

Har - minc - hat to - jás - ból csak egy csir - ke lett.
Out of all those eggs will come one lit - tle chick.

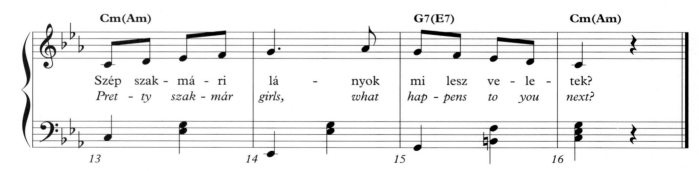

Szép szak - má - ri lá - nyok mi lesz ve - le - tek?
Pret - ty szak - már girls, what hap - pens to you next?

This song, in common with many Hungarian folk-songs, compares the life of young girls with growth in nature.

The dance (page 53) can be simplified as a circle dance with partners holding hands at shoulder level in a circle.

bars 1–8   8 csárdás steps to the right.

bars 9–16   8 csárdás steps to the left.

bars 1–8   8 rida steps to the right.

bars 9–16   8 rida steps to the left. Dancers drop hands.

bars 1–8   8 turning rida steps to the right.

bars 9–16   8 turning rida steps to the left.

Pünkösd napja

Whitsun

With marked rhythm

Traditional song
English words and accompaniment by Jean Gilbert

(Dance speed ♩ = 108)

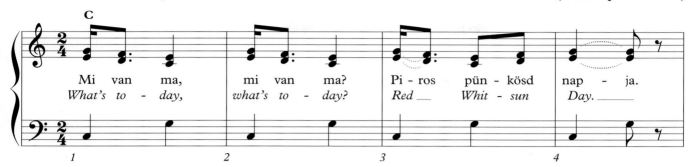

Mi van ma,   mi van ma?   Pi - ros   pün - kösd   nap - ja.
What's to - day,   what's to - day?   Red   Whit - sun   Day.

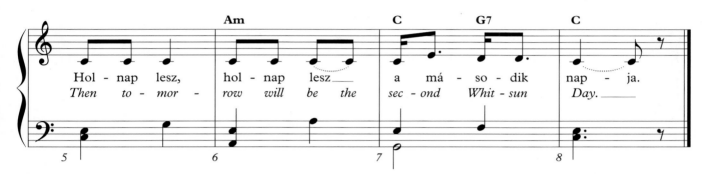

Hol - nap lesz,   hol - nap lesz   a má - so - dik   nap - ja.
Then to - mor - row will be the   sec - ond Whit - sun   Day.

Katona jól megtartsd,
lovadnak kantárát,
ne tiporja ne tapossa
a pünkösdi rózsát.

Hold your horse, hold your horse,
soldier, hold him steady,
so that he does not crush
the Whitsun red rose.

The Whitsun Queen

The election of the Whitsun Queen is an important event of this festival. A silken canopy is held over the Queen as she and her retinue walk from house to house. At each visit the Queen is 'lifted' while everyone chants 'This is how the flax must grow'. The Hungarian climate favours the growth of flax which is used for the manufacture of linen. There used to be a Whitsun King as well but this custom is now extinct.

This song is sung by children at Whitsun ('pünkösd') when they visit houses of friends and neighbours. They hold branches of flowering trees which are decorated with red, white and green ribbons, and ask permission to dance.

The dance

The children form a circle holding hands. There is no set formation or sequence of steps. It is best to teach the steps as described first (see page 57) and then to choreograph them into a simple dance. Here is one arrangement:

bars 1–4   4 csárdás steps to the right.

bars 5–8   4 csárdás steps to the left.

bars 1–4   4 rida steps to the right.

bars 5–8   4 rida steps to the left. Children drop hands.

bars 1–4   4 turning rida steps to the right.

bars 5–8   4 turning rida steps to the left. Children join hands again.

bars 1–4   4 csárdás steps to the right

bars 5–8   4 csárdás steps to the left.

Búj-búj zöld ág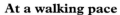
Through the branches

Traditional singing game
English words and accompaniment by Jean Gilbert

At a walking pace

Búj - búj zöld ág zöld le - ve - lecs - ke,
Through the branch - es, green, green branch - es,

nyit - va van az a - rany ka - pu Csak búj - ja - tok raj - ta.
see the gold - en gate is op - en, you can go through now.

Nyisd ki ró - zsám, ka - pu - dat, ka - pu - dat, hadd ke -
Op - en my dear, gold - en gate, gold - en gate, to your

- rül - jem vá - ra - dat, vá - ra - dat. Szi - ta - szi - ta pén - tek,
cas - tle let me walk all a - round. Siev - ing on a Fri - day,

sze - re - lem csü - tör - tök, dob szer - da. -da.
lov - ing on a Thurs - day, drum Wednes - day. -day.

This little song is really about the springtime, which is when it is most often sung and played in Hungary.

The game is similar to our own 'Oranges and Lemons'. The children walk in a line going under the arches, each made by two children with hands joined and held high to form an arch. At the end of the song, 'Dob szerda' ('drum Wednesday'), the arch children lower their hands to catch one of the other children walking through. The game ends when all the walkers have been caught.

The arches

There can be one or more arches, spaced out, according to the number of children and how the game is organized. Each pair of children faces front, inside hands joined and held high.

The walkers

Each child in the line holds hands with the child in front and the one behind. The first child puts the right hand forward and the left hand back to take hands. The next child puts the left hand forward and the right hand back and so on down the line. Alternatively each child can put both hands on the shoulders of the one in front. They walk forward stepping on the beat and starting with the right foot.

Hungarian dance steps (one beat of the music for each movement)

One-step csárdás (chardash)

♪ With slightly bent knees take a small step with the right foot to the right.

♩ Close left foot to right foot.

The movement should be done from the knees. There should be no up and down movement of the body.

Rida (Reedoa) step

♪ With slightly bent knees, cross the right foot over the left, and step, body weight on the right foot, left heel raised.

♩ Small step to the left with the left foot, keeping the heel raised.

To change direction, the left foot crosses over the right, body weight on the left.

Turning rida

The step is performed turning on the spot, girls with hands on hips, boys with hands clasped behind. Four steps complete a circle.

Foot-swinging step

♪ Slight spring on right foot and at the same time lift the left leg bending the knee. The leg swings from the knee to the right.

♩ Hop and swing the leg to the left.

♩ Spring with feet together.

♩ Pause.

Repeat with the other foot in the opposite direction.

For lists of other resources see page 118.

Czech Republic

Česká Republika

The land which is now the Czech Republic used to be part of the country known as Czechoslovakia, but in January 1993 the two parts of the country, Czech and Slovak, split up to become two separate republics.

The Czech lands cover the old regions of Bohemia, Moravia and part of Silesia in the centre of Europe. This is an area of great mountains and lush rolling hills. There are ski slopes in the Bohemian mountains and famous health resorts such as Karlovy Vary and Mariánské Lázně where people come to bathe in the mineral waters.

The beautiful old city of Prague, the capital, lies in the centre of Bohemia in the plain called the Bohemian Basin. The river Vltava flows through Prague on its way to join the river Elbe and thence through Germany to the North Sea. The Bohemian composer Smetana wrote a suite of

pieces called *My Country* (*'Má Vlast'*) which contains a melody called 'The Moldau', the German name for the Vltava. The music conveys the sound of this wide, peaceful river as it ebbs and flows through the countryside.

Most of the country has cold, snowy winters and warm summers. In general the lowlands are much warmer and drier than the mountainous areas. Crops of sugar beet, corn, hops, flax and fruit are grown in the fertile, sheltered river valleys. The famous Czech fruit dumplings originated in the fruit-growing districts. The recipe on page 60 shows you how to make plum dumplings with poppy seeds.

History

The Czech lands were first populated by Celts as early as 500 BC. By about AD 500, various Slavonic tribes had settled in the Bohemian part of what is now the Czech Republic. The most powerful of these were the Čechové (Czechs).

Bohemia began to rise in importance during the tenth century. One of the best-known rulers of the time was Prince Václav, the legendary 'Good King Wenceslas'. He spread Christianity among the people and became the patron saint of Bohemia after his death.

King Wenceslas

The country flourished under the rule of Charles IV (1346–78). Charles was crowned Holy Roman Emperor and Bohemia became the centre of the Roman Empire, with Prague the Empire's leading city. In 1526 Bohemia and Moravia became part of the Austrian Empire. They regained their independence after the First World War in 1918 when the Republic of Czechoslovakia was formed. This lasted until 1993 when the Czech and Slovak lands became separate republics.

The present population is mainly Czech and Moravian, people of Slavonic origin, but there are small minorities of Romanies (gypsies) and groups from bordering countries.

Some famous people

Composers

Bedřich Smetana (1828–84) is known to the Czech people as the founder of Czech national music. His symphonic suite *Má Vlast* ('My Country' or 'My Fatherland') and opera *The Bartered Bride* are performed all over the world.

Antonín Dvořák (1841–1904) is probably best known for his *Slavonic Dances* based on folk tunes from Bohemia, and his *'New World'* Symphony which he composed during a trip to America. This has a beautiful recurring theme which quotes a Negro spiritual known as 'Going home'.

Leoš Janáček (1854–1928) is best known for his operas including *Jenufa*, his masterpiece, and *The Cunning Little Vixen*.

Literature

Jaroslav Hašek (1854–1928) wrote *The Good Soldier Schweik*, probably the most famous book written by a Czech writer.
Karel Čapek (1890–1938) and **Franz Kafka** (1883–1924), are both renowned world writers.

Main crops:

wheat, barley, sugar beet, potatoes, hops

People's jobs:

Agricultural 9%

Industrial 48%

Other 43%

Main industries:

cars, metals, metal products, chemicals

59

Language 25

The official language is Czech, a Slav language.

English	Czech
one	jeden
two	dva
three	tři
four	čtyři
five	pět
six	šest
seven	sedm
eight	osm
nine	devět
ten	deset
good morning	dobré ráno
good day	dobrý den
good evening	dobrý večer
hello!	ahoj!
how are things?	jak se daři?
fine	dobře
thank you	děkuji
please	prosím
yes	ano
no	ne
goodbye	nashledanou

Suggestions for language activities can be found on page 7.

Food and drink

The day begins early for most Czechs so breakfast is little more than a cup of coffee or plain tea and some fresh bread, with jam, cheese or salami. The main meal is eaten at lunchtime, and a smaller meal, traditionally of cold meats and bread, in the evening.

There is always time for the daily ritual of coffee and cake. Like the Austrians who once ruled over them, the Czechs have a very sweet tooth. Coffee is usually drunk black, and tea weak and without milk.

The highlight of every Czech feast is roast goose served with potato dumplings and 'sauerkraut' or pickled cabbage. It is a great favourite for special occasions like New Year's Day, weddings and festival celebrations. Fish from the rivers and hundreds of beautiful lakes in south Bohemia is served in a variety of ways. At Christmas, carp is the traditional dish rather than poultry. Good

wine comes from South Moravia but the king of all drinks has always been Czech beer.

Svestkové knedlíky s mákem
(Plum dumplings with poppy seed)

This recipe comes from the Elbe basin

1kg plums
800g coarse flour
300g soft cottage cheese
150g butter

3 eggs
300ml milk
salt
whipped cream

Sift the flour, then beat in the eggs, cottage cheese and milk to make a dough.

Roll out and cut into squares.

Place a plum on each square, then bring up the edges of the dough and seal firmly.

Cook in boiling water for 8-12 minutes according to size.

Sprinkle with minced poppy seed, sugar and warmed butter and decorate with whipped cream.

Krkonoše bramborové placky
(Krkonoše potato pancakes)

This recipe comes from the Giant Mountains, where these pancakes are served for tea.

The following quantities are intended for 4 substantial helpings but, in school, try making (about 20) tiny pancakes for the children to taste.

1kg potatoes
2 eggs
6 tablespoons coarse flour

4 cloves garlic
marjoram, salt and pepper to season
oil or cooking fat

Peel and grate the raw potatoes.

Add the crushed garlic, seasoning, flour and eggs and mix thoroughly.

Heat some oil or fat in a frying pan, spoon a little batter into it, spreading it out fairly thinly, and fry till the pancake is crisp on both sides.

Serve while still hot.

The children can be involved in preparing the batter but the frying in hot oil should be done by an adult.

Art and craft

Bohemia is probably most famous for its glass products — vases, goblets, bowls and ornaments. The Czech Republic exports many other craft objects including handmade toys, dolls, china, wood carvings, jewellery and lace.

Decorated eggs

The custom of decorating eggshells and hard-boiled eggs, already widespread in Bohemia by the fourteenth century, has led to a variety of decorative techniques for which Easter eggs from Bohemia and Moravia have become famous. The eggs are decorated in various ways: with batik, scraping, etching with acid, pasting with straw. The results are real little works of art!

The children could try simpler methods with hard-boiled eggs.

1 Just paint straight on with a fine brush using poster paint, ready-made or prepared with powder, or use felt-tipped pens. The eggs can then be varnished to give a glossy finish and preserve the paint.

2 The eggs can be dyed a single colour by hard-boiling them with onion skins (yellow), beetroot (red), spinach leaves (green) or a few drops of food dye. When dry, a pattern can then be painted on with a suitably contrasting colour(s), using a stencil cut from paper if this is helpful.

3 Plain hard-boiled eggs can be dipped and coated in paraffin wax. A pattern can then be scratched right through the wax to the shell so that when the egg is dipped in cold dye and the wax melted off in a warm oven, the pattern will remain. A more elaborate pattern can be obtained by scratching and dipping several times before the wax is finally melted off.

Suggestions for general classroom activities can be found on page 6.

Folk costume

The variety of costumes reflects the type of region, lowland or mountainous, and the influence of neighbouring countries. Cut and ornamentation may be specific to a particular district or even village, but a common feature is the rich embroidery that adorns almost every piece of clothing belonging to the costume.

The costumes illustrated in the colour section show typical features of dress worn in Bohemia.

Festivals

In common with other European countries, many of the Czech festivals mark the different seasons of the year. Folk ceremonies and customs were always taken very seriously in the past. Quite a number have been preserved though their original meaning has been lost.

The curious medieval custom of Easter 'swishing' is still commonly observed. Traditionally, women and girls were swished, to make them healthier and thus more attractive. The switches, made of young willow twigs, were believed to have magical powers. Today they can still be bought before Easter (Velikonoce) in Prague itself, and the decorated Easter eggs with which the girls reward the young men are on sale everywhere. In some areas boys and girls douse each other with water, a relic of ancient spring cleansing ceremonies.

Maypoles are decorated for May Day (Svátek práce). Sometimes small ones are placed by boys outside the houses of their girlfriends. If they are accepted, the girl will become the boy's partner to dance round the big maypole in the village.

Bringing in the harvest, one of the most important events for the farming population, is still celebrated today with spectacular harvest festivals. These culminate in feasts and fairs, bringing the farming season to a close.

At the end of winter, children carry a figure representing winter (death) away from the village. Death Sunday (Smrtná neděla) occurs a fortnight before Easter and is still observed in parts of Moravia. A doll, dressed up in the folk costume of the village as an old woman or goddess of winter, is carried in a procession down to the river and thrown into the water. Everyone watches the doll, called 'Smrtka' or 'Morena', float away, then they return to the village to dance and celebrate the end of winter.

This simple folk song lends itself to solo and small group singing.

Smrtná neděla
Tell me Death Sunday

Traditional song from Moravia
English words by Jean Gilbert

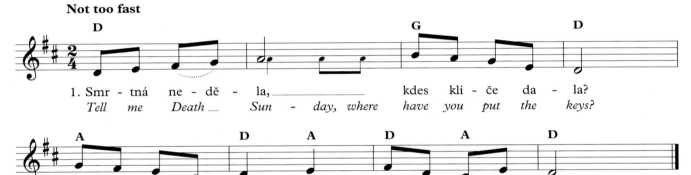

Not too fast

1. Smr - tná ne - dě - la, _____ kdes klí - če da - la?
Tell me Death Sun - day, where have you put the keys?

'Da - la jsem je, da - la kvě - tne ne - dě - li.'
'I have giv - en them to Flow - er Sun - day.'

2. Květná neděla,
kdes klíče dala?
'Dala jsem je, dala
květným pondělkům.'

3. Květný pondělku,
kdes klíče poděl?
'Poděl jsem je, poděl
zeleným čturtkum.'

4. Zelený čturtku,
kdes klíče poděl?
'Poděl jsem je, poděl
svatému Jiří.'

5. Svaty Jiří vstal,
zemi odmýkal,
aby tráva růstla,
tráva zelená.

2. *Tell me, Flower Sunday,*
where have you put the keys?
'I have given them to
Flower Monday.'

3. *Tell me, Flower Monday,*
where have you put the keys?
'I have given them to
Green Thursday.'

4. *Tell me, Green Thursday,*
where have you put the keys?
'I have passed them on to
good Saint George.'

5. *Saint George got up and*
he unlocked the earth,
so that all the green grass,
green grass could grow.

Tancůj, tancůj
Dancing, dancing

Traditional Slovakian dance
English words by Jean Gilbert
Accompaniment adapted from J. Kvapil

Lively

(Dance speed ♩ = 144)

INTRODUCTION

Tan - cůj,
Danc - ing,

tan - cůj
danc - ing,
vyk - rú - caj,
joy - ful - ly,
vyk - rú - caj,
joy - ful - ly,
len mi
mind my
piec - ku
stave, go

nez - rú - caj,
care - ful - ly,
nez - rú - caj,
care - ful - ly,
dob - rá
we need
piec - ka
staves for
na zi - mu,
win - ter - time,

na zi - mu,
win - ter - time,
ne - má
not all
kaž - dý
folks have
pe - ri - nu,
feath - er beds,
pe - ri - nu.
feath - er beds.

63

Suggested accompaniment

Tambourine (B section):

This dance song in fact comes from Slovakia but it is also very popular, particularly at festival times, in Moravia on the Czech side of the border. It has a number of other verses which have not been included here.

The dance 28

This is a couple dance, with couples facing one another in short, staggered rows. They take a csárdás hold to begin with. (Movements are explained on page 65.)

Figure 1

bars 1–8   8 shunting steps going to the left and then to the right of each partner and always returning to place.

bars 9–16   Retaining hold, move to boy's left and girl's right with: step, close, step, close with a stamp.

Repeat 3 times in alternate directions.

bars 17–24   Large clap (hands moving like clashing cymbals).

Link right arms and walk round with 14 smooth steps. Boy's free arm is raised; girl's free arm is down following line of skirt.

bars 25–32   Repeat all to left, but with 12 small steps and a stamp with the left foot on last beat.

Figure 2

bars 1–8   Hands on waist, facing partners, each moving to the left.

Step, close, step, shunting right leg across left.

Repeat to right, left, right.

Repeat Figure 1 to complete the dance.

bars 9–16   Hop on right foot placing left toe inverted to the side, slightly forward.

Hop on right foot with left heel to the side.

Repeat 7 times on alternate feet.

Boy's arms are raised and girl's are in a low V.

bars 17–32   As for Figure 1.

Movements

Csárdás hold   Girl places hands on boy's shoulders. Boy places hands on girl's shoulder blades underneath her arms. Arms are straight.

Shunting step   Shunt or slide forward with both feet together. Shunt back again to place.

Kominík 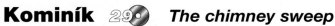 *The chimney sweep*

Traditional singing game from Nymburk, Bohemia
English words and accompaniment by Jean Gilbert

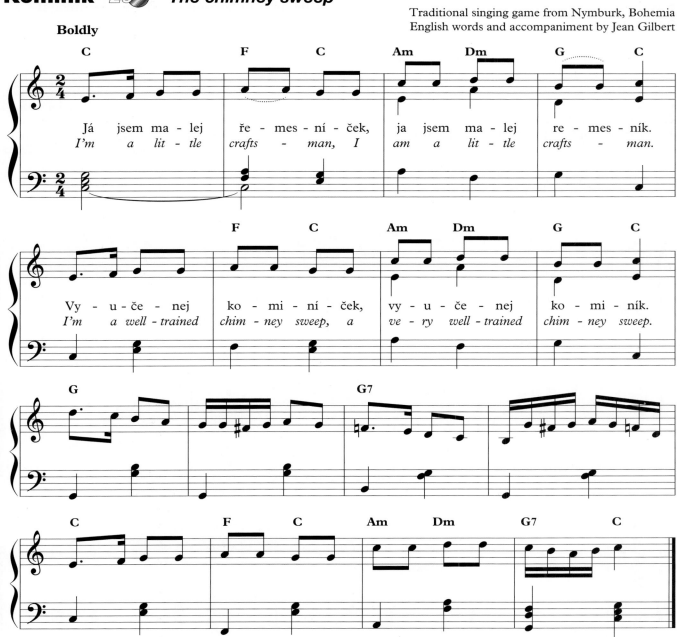

Boldly

Já jsem ma - lej   ře - mes - ní - ček,   ja jsem ma - lej   re - mes - ník.
I'm   a   lit - tle   crafts - man, I   am   a   lit - tle   crafts - man.

Vy - u - če - nej   ko - mi - ní - ček,   vy - u - če - nej   ko - mi - ník.
I'm   a   well - trained   chim - ney   sweep,   a   ve - ry   well - trained   chim - ney   sweep.

Suggested accompaniment

Tambourine plays on the last 8 bars:

This game is a favourite among young children. It can be danced by boys, girls, or a mixed group.

The children form a line led by the chimney-sweep who carries a besom (a yard broom made of dark twigs). They hold each other by the waist and perform a sequence of steps as agreed or called, for example:

● walking steps only
● step-hop
● step-hop raising knee very high
● step-hop extending leg sideways

● polka step
● hopping on haunches

The chimney-sweep makes all kinds of patterns with the besom: figure-of-eight, horizontal circle overhead, changing the besom from one hand to the other hand, and so on. He/she must lead the line around the room in such a way as to be able to tap the last person in the line with the besom. The last person tries to avoid being touched or 'caught'. However, when the sweep succeeds in tapping the last dancer in the line, that child gets the besom and becomes the new leader.

A besom can be improvised, but if nothing is available, or if preferred, a hand will do and the sweep can lead the line with claps.

Švec a kovář 30
Cobbler and blacksmith's dance

Traditional craft dance from Moravia
collected by Hedy Fromings,
who learnt the dance from the group 'Kasàva', in Moravia.
Accompaniment by Jean Gilbert

The dance

There are many dances which feature various occupations, such as this craft dance from North Moravia.

The children take partners and form a circle, the girl on the outside. During the introduction they take a 'rounded' ballroom hold, the boy holding the girl's right hand, fingers pointing downwards.

A 16 polka steps. The girl finishes on the inside of the circle facing the boy, both down on right knee, left knee raised.

B With the left fist on the raised knee, make the awl movement 4 times, pushing into the left palm with the right forefinger. (The awl is the cobbler's sharp instrument for making holes.) Then hammer the knee 4 times, 'stitch' by pointing forefingers to partner 4 times and 'tie and pull the thread' to finish.

Repeat, standing up on the last beat.

C 16 polka steps, the boy stopping on the outside of the circle.

D The partners stretch hands towards each other; the girl has both palms turned upwards, the right hand on top of the left while the boy has his left hand under the girl's hands. He swings his right arm down, round, then overhead to hit her palm, then he turns her top hand over. She returns the swing-hit while he repeats her hand movements. (This indicates payment for the shoes.)

Repeat both.

E Facing each other, clap own hands then partner's hands while step-hopping 8 times into the centre, the girl going backwards.

Repeat to places, the boy going backwards. (The foot is always raised in front of the body for the hop.)

F The dance finishes with a polka sequence. With an open hold couples take 2 polka steps forward, then the girl turns under the boy's raised right arm. Repeat . . . then finally the girl makes only the turns as they dance away, the boy making stamp-steps, swishing the girl's skirt as she turns. Repeat 'F' music as necessary.

The polka step in this dance has a smooth or rolling quality. The movement should be low rather than high as in other kinds of polkas. It can finish with a small flick step on the last beat. Simple skipping steps can be substituted for the polka for younger children. The dance can be simplified by just dancing the first two sections in the order ABA.

For lists of other resources see page 118.

Germany

Deutschland

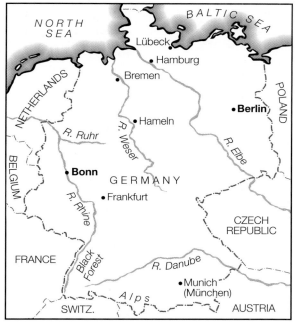

Germany lies in the middle of Europe, a large, powerful and important country, a land of high mountains, forests, deep river valleys and broad plains.

It has the biggest population of any of the western European countries including a large minority of 'Gastarbeiter' (immigrant workers). They came mainly from Turkey but also from Spain, Greece, Italy, Austria, former Yugoslavia and Asia.

In the south of Germany some of the highest mountain peaks rise in the Alps, which form a natural border with Switzerland and Austria, where lifestyles are very similar. Cattle in these parts are moved to higher pastures for the hot summer months and return in the autumn for shelter during the harsh icy winters.

In central Germany the mountains give way to high fertile plains, valleys and thick forests. Here the winters are less severe and the summers hot and sunny. The northern lowlands are quite different. The weather is mild and wet and the land flat with gravelly heathland, shallow lakes and marshes. Sandy stretches along the Baltic coast are popular with holiday-makers, but the water is never very warm.

In the west of Germany major industrial towns were established on or near the rivers Rhine and Ruhr, which provided water for industries and were important as waterways for the transport of heavy goods. Sailing boats, water buses and cruise ships filled with tourists also travel on these wide rivers. The Rhine valley is particularly popular with tourists. It is lined with beautiful little towns and there are turreted castles built high on hills overlooking the land, just like the ones in fairy-tale books. Some of Germany's famous white wines come from the vineyards along the sheltered slopes of the valley.

The strange legend of the Pied Piper comes from Hameln (Hamelin town in Robert Browning's poem) where

'The river Weser, deep and wide,
'Washes its wall on the southern side.'

Every Sunday at noon during the summer months, the story is played out by actors and children near the rat catcher's house, the 'Rattenfängerhaus'.

History

Ancient tribes from the north of Europe, including Franks and Goths, migrated south, some of them reaching the Rhine and Danube rivers. When the Romans invaded in the first century AD, they named them 'Germani' and their land 'Germania'.

Some of these tribes migrated west into Gaul (now France), Spain and Italy, helping to bring about the collapse of the Roman Empire. Power eventually passed to Charlemagne, the great Frankish ruler, when he was crowned Emperor of the Romans in AD 800. After his death, his empire was divided among his three grandsons. The lands east of the Rhine river became what is now Germany.

For a long time after this, Germany was divided into small states, each with its own ruler. It was not until 1871 that they came together under Bismarck, 'the Iron Chancellor'. Prussia's king then became the first Kaiser (or emperor) of the newly created German Empire with Berlin as its capital city.

By the early twentieth century Germany was a major industrial nation. During this century Germany fought and lost two world wars. After the First World War, the National Socialist Party (the Nazis) led by Adolf Hitler promised to make Germany great again. Their programme eventually resulted in the Second World War, the most terrible in history. The wartime suffering of the peoples of Europe was made even worse by the Nazi policy of exterminating Jews, gypsies and others who were regarded as racially inferior. Germany was again defeated and in 1945 the country was divided into East and West Germany, each with its own government.

In the late 1980s great political changes swept across Europe. The Berlin Wall that symbolized the division of the nation was knocked down, Germany was reunited and free elections were held in 1990. Berlin became the official capital of Germany once again.

Language

German belongs to the Germanic group of European languages. It is the national language of Germany and Austria, one of the four national languages of Switzerland and one of the main cultural languages of the Western world.

English	German
one	eins
two	zwei
three	drei
four	vier
five	fünf
six	sechs
seven	sieben
eight	acht
nine	neun
ten	zehn
good morning	guten Morgen
good day	guten Tag
good evening	guten Abend
how are things?	wie geht's?
fine	danke, gut
thank you	danke schön
please	bitte
yes	ja
no	nein
goodbye	auf Wiedersehen

German and English are related languages and share many identical or similar words: 'Land' (land), 'Buch' (book), 'Maus' (mouse), 'Wolle' (wool), etc.

Some English words are taken directly from the German:

dachshund (dog), rottweiler (dog), ersatz (artificial), kaput (broken), kindergarten (nursery school), rucksack (shoulder bag), etc.
Can the children list any more?

Suggestions for further language activities can be found on page 7.

Some famous people

Literature

Goethe (1749–1832) was Europe's most celebrated writer of the time. His most famous work, *Faust*, is the story of a man who makes a pact with the Devil.

The Brothers Grimm (1785–1863) wrote a collection of fairy-tales including 'Snow White' and 'Little Red Riding Hood'.

Bertolt Brecht (1896–1956) was one of Germany's leading dramatists. His major works include *The Threepenny Opera* with music by Kurt Weill.

Science

Johannes Kepler (1571–1630) was an astronomer and mathematician. His theories helped Sir Isaac Newton understand the principles of gravity.

Gabriel Fahrenheit (1686–1736) invented the mercury thermometer and devised the temperature scale that bears his name.

Fritz Haber (1868–1955) invented the process for making artificial fertilizers.

Albert Einstein (1879–1955) invented the theory of relativity. He was one of the greatest scientists of all time.

Music

Many of the Western world's most famous composers have been German. They include **J. S. Bach** (1685–1750), **Handel** (1685–1759), **Beethoven** (1770–1827), **Mendelssohn** (1809–47), **Schumann** (1810–56), **Wagner** (1813–83) and **Brahms** (1833–97).

Among twentieth-century composers, **Kurt Weill** (1900–50) is best known for his work for the theatre, particularly his songs and music for *The Threepenny Opera*.

Carl Orff (1895–1982) was a composer and a teacher. His works include *Carmina Burana* and *Schulwerk*, a method of class music teaching using glockenspiels and other percussion instruments.

Philosophy

Immanuel Kant (1724–1804) has had a lasting influence on Western thought.

Karl Marx (1818–83) was a radical thinker who advocated the common ownership of land and industry. His most important work was *Das Kapital*.

Technology

Johann Gutenberg (c.1397–1468) invented the printing press. A bible known as the Gutenberg Bible was among his first printed works.

Main crops:

potatoes, sugar beet, barley, wheat

Main industries:

transport equipment, machinery, metals, metal products, chemicals

People's jobs:

Agricultural	4%
Industrial	40%
Other	56%

Food and drink

The two foods for which Germany is probably best known are bread and sausages. In some parts of the country there are more than two hundred types of bread to choose from. Most of these are baked from dark rye flour rather than the wheat flour we use to bake white and wholemeal bread.

Every butcher's shop is festooned with a wide variety of sausages. 'Bratwurst', made of pork and veal, can be fried or grilled. 'Currywurst' is very spicy and delicious served with a bread roll and a curry flavoured tomato sauce. The famous 'Frankfurters', made from lean pork, are often eaten with 'sauerkraut' (pickled cabbage), or in lentil, pea or potato soup. Because of the demand for pork in sausages and other dishes, pig rearing is an important part of farming.

Among other regional specialities, perhaps the best-known gateau is the 'Schwarzwälder Kirschtorte', the Black Forest cherry cake.

The day begins early with a small breakfast of crusty rolls with butter and jam, cheese or ham and coffee. Children often prefer milk, hot chocolate or fruit juice and they take a sandwich with them to school to eat as a second breakfast. After school closes (between 12 noon and 1 pm) they go home for 'Mittagessen' (midday dinner). This is traditionally the largest meal of the day. It might consist of a thick soup followed by meat, frequently pork or veal, with vegetables. A popular dessert is 'Milchreis', a rice dish cooked with milk and sultanas and flavoured with cinnamon. Supper is a much lighter meal with cold meat, bread and salad or just sandwiches.

Germans are fond of good beer, much of which comes from the many local breweries that are dotted around the country. There are also excellent wines to choose from. Riesling and Liebfraumilch wines are great favourites.

Aufschnitt (Cold meats)

This dish is based on a selection of sausages ('Wurst') and cold meats. It is usually the main dish of the evening meal ('Abendbrot').

Ask the children to contribute to the following:

100g each of (sliced) German salami, cervelat, ham, liver sausage ('Leberwurst') and beer sausage ('Bierwurst'), or whatever is available locally.

3 pickled medium sized gherkins

1 hard-boiled egg (sliced)

fresh parsley

Display the meats attractively on a large plate or dish and decorate with the slices of egg, gherkins and parsley.

For a special meal at school, serve with different kinds of German bread like rye bread ('Roggenbrot') or 'Pumpernickel', which is a dark, almost black rye bread, often pre-packed in slices. Add a prepared salad.

Marmorkuchen (Marble cake)

This is quite easy to make and can be cut up into small slices for tasting.

250g salted butter or margarine	juice and rind of 1 lemon
250g sugar	50g cocoa
500g flour	30g (extra) sugar
4 eggs	125ml milk
2 teaspoons baking powder	

Cream the butter and sugar.

Add the beaten eggs one by one. Mix well until smooth.

Add the lemon juice and rind. Mix well.

Sieve the flour and baking powder and add to the mixture.

Stir in the milk.

Put one third of the mixture into a separate bowl and add cocoa, extra sugar and 2 tablespoons extra milk.

Grease a cake tin (preferably a special ring-shaped tin):

Put in half the light-coloured mixture.

Add the cocoa mixture.

Pour over the rest of the light mixture.

Swirl a fork through the dough to produce a marbling effect.

Bake for 60 minutes at gas mark 4, 190° C (375° F).

When cool, turn out onto wire rack and dust with sieved icing sugar. Cut when completely cool. (This cake can be frozen.)

Art and craft

Autumn lanterns

At the time of Martinfest (St Martin's festival), see page 74, children make their own lanterns to carry in procession during the festival. The lanterns carry a candle or night-light but, in school, any craft work involving a naked flame is not recommended unless very carefully supervised.

A simple lantern can be made using thick coloured paper and the round lid of a cheese spread box.

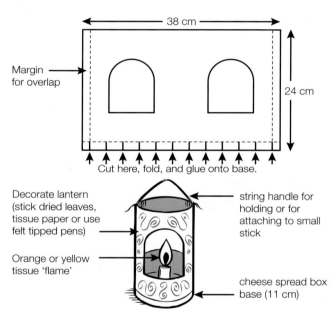

38 cm

Margin for overlap

24 cm

Cut here, fold, and glue onto base.

Decorate lantern (stick dried leaves, tissue paper or use felt tipped pens)

string handle for holding or for attaching to small stick

Orange or yellow tissue 'flame'

cheese spread box base (11 cm)

A sturdier alternative would be to use a metal lid and heavyweight foil and, with care, a small night light for real! Instead of 'windows' punch a pattern of holes using different sized knitting needles.

Suggestions for general class activities can be found on page 6.

Folk costume

Germany is a large country. The costumes are varied, and many reflect the styles of neighbouring countries. Nowadays they are mainly worn on special occasions such as local celebrations, festivals and religious events.

Throughout the country there are numerous ways of wearing bodices, blouses, skirts and aprons, but it is the hats that are an interesting and important feature of German costume. They can be tall, small, ribbonned, veiled or elaborately decorated. Each region and village will have a different style. The men's costumes tend to be similar in style with variations on knee breeches, waistcoats, jackets, shirts and hats.

The illustrations in the colour section show costumes typical of Bavaria where the men's breeches are replaced by leather shorts, 'Lederhosen', common to both Germany and Austria. The Munich Octoberfest provides a unique opportunity for all Bavarians to wear their folk costume and is a good place for visitors to see the different varieties of Bavarian costume.

Festivals

Festivals, fairs and celebrations have always been an important part of German tradition.

Country-wide celebrations are linked with Christmas, Easter and the New Year. 'Fasching', the season of Carnival, includes street fairs, parades, masked balls and many other events which take place in the weeks leading up to Ash Wednesday.

There are Marksmen's Festivals ('Schützenfeste') all over Germany. These festivals originated five or six hundred years ago when marksmen, rather than knights, became responsible for the protection of towns and villages. Contests which were held at regular intervals to keep the marksmen in top form have now developed into folk festivals in which everyone participates.

Particular parts of the country are famous for their festivals, for example Bavaria. Here, in Munich, the two-week October Fair ('Oktoberfest') is the world's most famous beer festival, dating back to 1810, to the engagement party of King Ludwig and his future bride Theresa. It is now the occasion for drinking, feasting and enjoying the fine parades, markets and pageants.

In the German Alps, cattle are moved to higher pastures for the summer months ('Almauftrieb') and return for winter shelter in the autumn ('Almabtrieb'). Both occasions are important to farmers and the local community. Much preparation is needed, for the cattle and their minders will be away for several months. In the spring, herdsmen assemble the long procession of animals with their ringing bells and set out for the huts high in the mountains where the animals will be tended and where butter and cheese will be made for autumn marketing. In the autumn when the cattle return, sleek and fat, there is great rejoicing with elaborate welcome-home suppers and music and dancing.

St Martin's Festival ('Martinfest') is a children's festival, celebrated throughout the Rhineland and in Bavaria on 11 November. It honours St Martin, friend of children and patron of the poor, and also Martin Luther, leader of the Reformation in Germany. The Eve is characterized by a children's lantern procession and the Day by feasting on roast goose. The procession is led by a man on horseback representing St Martin and showing how he tore his cloak to share it with a beggar. The children follow, singing and carrying their lanterns.

Laterne, Laterne 32
The lanterns shine brightly

Traditional song
English words by Jean Gilbert

Moderato

La - ter - ne, La - ter - ne! Son - ne Mond und
The lan - terns shine bright - ly like the sun and

Ster - ne! Bren - ne auf mein Licht! Bren - ne auf mein Licht! Es
moon and stars! Bright - ly shine my light! bright - ly shine my light! Our

scha - det uns - rer La - ter - ne nicht. Vor Ham - burg, Lü - beck,
lan - terns are safe through - out the night. In Ham - burg, Lü - beck,

Bre - men, da brau - chen wir uns nicht zu schä - men.
Bre - men, there's no - thing to com - pare with them.

Uns - re La - ter - ne bunt und schön, kann man weit von fer - ne sehn.
Mul - ti - col - oured lan - terns shin - ing bright, you can see their dis - tant light.

74

Barbara Lester, from whom this song was collected, remembers taking part in these processions as a child. She says that not once does she remember the lanterns catching fire!

Suggestions for making lanterns are given on page 73.

Suggested accompaniment

Last 4 bars: triangle

The tune could be played by descant recorders throughout.

There are many Spring festivals ('Frühlingsfeste') in different parts of Germany. This nineteenth-century folk-song celebrates the end of winter. It is a round in three voices and is sung throughout Germany.

Es tönen die Lieder
The spring songs are sounding

Traditional words and music
English words by Jean Gilbert

Es tö - nen die Lie - der, der Früh - ling kehrt
The spring songs are sound - ing, and birds they are

wie - der, es flö - tet der Hir - te auf sei - ner Schal -
sing - ing, the shep - herd will play on his lit - tle Schal -

- mei*: tra la la la la la la la, tra la la la la la la la!
- mey:

*The 'Schalmei' referred to in the German version is a *shawm*, an early member of the oboe family.

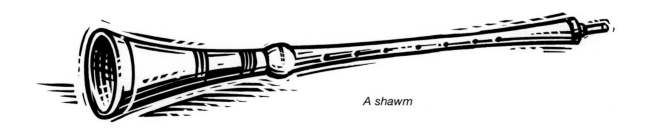

A shawm

75

Alle Vögel sind schon da

All the birds are here again

Traditional song
English words and accompaniment by Jean Gilbert

This well-known song greets the return of the birds in springtime.

2. Wie, sie alle lustig sind,
   flink und froh sich regen.
   Amsel, Drossel, Fink und Star
   und die ganze Vogelschar
   wünschen uns ein frohes Jahr,
   lauter Heil und Segen.

2. *All the birds sing cheerfully*
   hopping, flying freely.
   Blackbird, starling, finch and thrush,
   every flock and every bird
   wish us all a happy year,
   full of joy and gladness.

The tune itself is a clear example of a three-part melody: A B A. The tune for the first two lines is repeated in the last two lines. Ask the children to listen out for this feature. Divide them into two groups and let them work out how they would sing the first verse to illustrate the three-part form.

Older children could similarly work out an instrumental arrangement, for example:

bars 1–4	recorders
bars 5–8	xylophone/glockenspiel/chime bars
bars 9–12	recorders

Suggested accompaniment

The recording illustrates a simple accompaniment on the glockenspiel which could also be played on chime bars, metallophone or by recorders.

Brüderchen, komm tanz mit mir
Brother, come and dance with me

Traditional singing game from Thüringen
Adapted by Engelbert Humperdinck and
incorporated into his opera *Hänsel und Gretel*

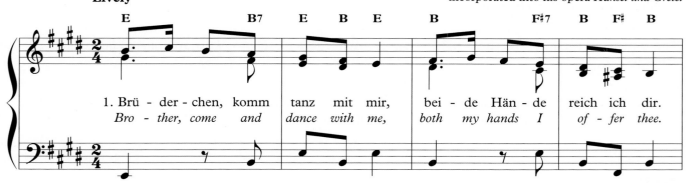

The last two lines of each verse are often translated as 'Right foot first, left foot then, roundabout and back again.'

The translated version given here reflects the German more closely to assist any related language activities.

Humperdinck (1854–1921) incorporated this children's rhyme into his opera *Hänsel and Gretel*. It is representative of both the folklore and folk-melodies of Germany and the words provide a guide to help the children choreograph a simple dance. They will also suggest percussion. Ask the children for their ideas.

Polka 36

Traditional music and dance

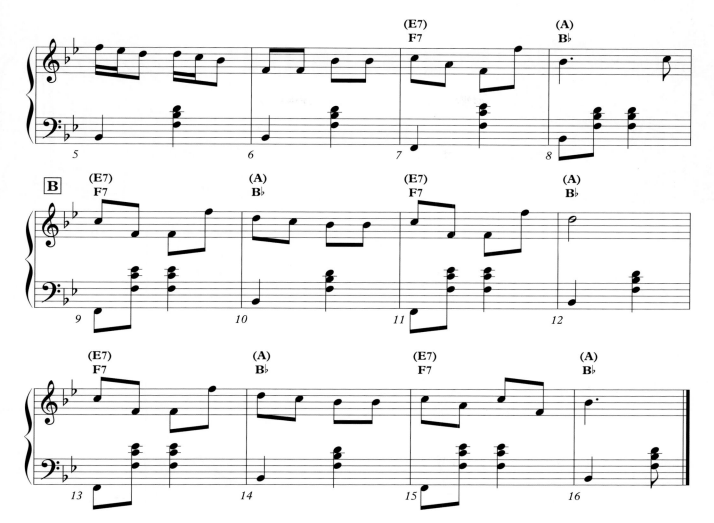

The style of German folk dances is as varied as the geography of the country itself and often reflects the dancing of neighbouring countries. Couple dances became popular in the south of Germany where the polka had crossed over from Bohemia in the Czech Republic.

The dance 36

Children choose a partner and face counter-clockwise in a circle, inside hands joined.

A	bars 1–4	Begin with foot furthest away from partner. 2 polkas forward with straight leg on hop. Clap hands on thighs, in front of face and 3 times on partner's hands.
A	bars 5–8	Repeat.
B	bars 9–12	Face partner. 1 side-step right and left, and repeat.

B	bars 13–16	Link right elbow with partner. 8 skips (twice round) and back to places. Or 4 polkas turning partner.

Steps

Polka	Step forward onto right foot, bring left foot up to right foot and step. Step onto right foot and hop, 'unfolding' left foot forward. Continue, stepping forward onto left foot. 1 polka step per bar.
Polka	For the turning polka use either a 'peasant' hold with boy's hands on girl's waist and girl's hands on boy's shoulders, or a 'ballroom' hold.
Side-step	Step to the right, bring left foot up and step left, right. Continue to the left. 1 side-step per bar.

For lists of other resources see page 118.

France

France

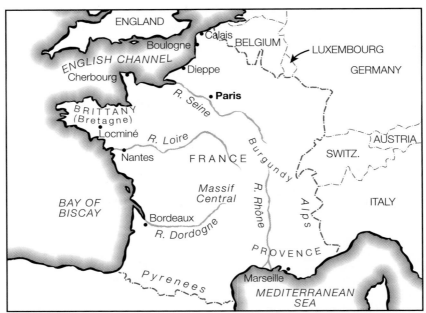

France, our nearest neighbour, is the largest country in Europe, though one of the least densely populated. Paris, the capital city, is situated on the river Seine in the north and is closer to London than many of our own big cities — Newcastle, for instance. It is regarded as one of the most beautiful cities in the world.

Because of the size of the country there is a great range of climate and scenery. There are areas of high mountains, dramatic river gorges and broad fertile plains. The regions and the people also have quite different traditions and life styles even now.

To the north of Paris the land is flat and the climate similar to that of England. This is one of the most important commercial and industrial areas in France. The region of Brittany, further west, has a very long coastline and many of its songs and dances are related to the traditions of fishermen. It is similar to the south-west of

England in that it has a separate language, just as some people in Cornwall can still speak Cornish. Farming is important because of the damp, mild climate. Buckwheat, one of the cereal crops grown here, is used for making Breton pancakes (crêpes). They are mentioned in the song 'Les gars de Locminé', and in the recipe section you can find out how to make them.

The south of France is quite different, with a much warmer climate and a coastline along the Mediterranean sea. This region known as Provence is an important tourist area for the French themselves and for other Europeans. The recipe for crudités on page 84 is the perfect cool, crisp starter for eating during the long, hot summers of the south.

The Pyrenees mountains, also in the south, separate France and Spain. In the east the high ranges of the Alps border Italy and Switzerland.

History

The most important event in the history of France, the French Revolution, is celebrated every year on 14 July. 'Le 14 Juillet' is a national holiday to commemorate the time when ordinary people all over France banded together against the king and queen and lords and ladies (the aristocrats) who they felt had an unfair share of the riches of the land, while they were becoming increasingly poor and hungry.

On this day in 1789, the people of Paris attacked the prison (the Bastille) and released the prisoners. This victory encouraged further revolts and led to the beheading of the king and the queen, the overthrow of the monarchy and the establishment of a republic. The song 'La Marseillaise' on page 85 became the anthem of the new republic.

The land we know as France was first settled by the Gauls, Celtic peoples from Central Europe, in about 1000 BC. Their descendants are found mainly in Brittany. By about 50 BC Julius Caesar had conquered the country and it remained part of the Roman Empire for 500 years until the Franks invaded from the east in the fifth century. Their king, Clovis, settled in Paris, and gave France its present name and capital city, but the language continued to be based on that of the Romans. By the end of the eighth century the Franks had taken over all of France except Brittany. The ruling king Charles went on to capture much of the Roman empire in the west. He was crowned Emperor by the Pope in the year 800 and became known as Charlemagne (Charles the Great).

During the Middle Ages, parts of northern and western France were claimed by English kings, the descendants of William of Normandy (William the Conqueror). A famous French woman, Joan of Arc, 'the Maid of Orleans', is remembered for helping to drive the English out of France.

After the Revolution, Napoleon Bonaparte, a young general, led the French armies to great victories. He was not only a military genius but also a great statesman. Although he was defeated at the Battle of Waterloo (1815), his reforms, for example, in education and the law, helped to make France a great European power. France retains this position today despite the suffering and devastation of two world wars in the twentieth century.

Language

French belongs to the Romance group of languages derived from Latin. It ranks with English as an international language.

English	French
one	un
two	deux
three	trois
four	quatre
five	cinq
six	six
seven	sept
eight	huit
nine	neuf
ten	dix
good morning	bonjour
good evening	bonsoir
how are things?	ça va?
fine	ça va
thank you	merci
please	s'il vous plaît *or* s'il te plaît *between family and friends*
yes	oui
no	non
goodbye	au revoir

Suggestions for language activities can be found on page 7.

Joan of Arc

Some famous people

Literature

Famous writers include **Molière** (1622–73), playwright, **Victor Hugo** (1802–85) who wrote *Les Misérables* and **Alexandre Dumas** (1802–70) who wrote *The Three Musketeers*. **Jean Cocteau** (1889–1963), poet, novelist and dramatist, was also a noted film director.

Science

Antoine Lavoisier (1743–94), known as the founder of modern chemistry, discovered oxygen. He was executed during the Revolution.

Louis Pasteur (1822–95) discovered that germs cause disease.

Antoine Becquerel (1852–1908) discovered radioactivity.

Music

There are many famous French composers, including
Hector Berlioz (1803–69),
Camille Saint-Saëns (1835–1921),
Georges Bizet (1838–75),
Claude Debussy (1862–1918),
Paul Dukas (1865–1935) and
Maurice Ravel (1875–1937).

Philosophy

René Descartes (1596–1650) influenced modern philosophy. He was also a great mathematician.

Jean-Jacques Rousseau (1712–78) coined the slogan, 'Liberty, Equality, Fraternity', adopted by the French Revolutionaries.

Art

Artists famous for their Impressionist paintings include
Camille Pissaro (1830–1903),
Paul Cézanne (1839–1906),
Claude Monet (1840–1926) and
Auguste Renoir (1841–1919).

Film

Famous figures in the world of film include the film-makers **René Clair**, **Jean Renoir** and **Alain Resnais**.

Main crops:

wheat, sugar beet, maize, barley, livestock, dairy products, wine

People's jobs:

Agricultural 5%

Industrial 28%

Other 67%

Main industries:

food products, chemical products, transport equipment, machinery, metals, metal products

Food and drink

Good food is important to all French people. They like to buy fresh local produce from the markets found in every town and great care is taken with cooking, whether at home or in restaurants.

Family festivals such as weddings always include a big meal when everyone sits down round a large table, out of doors if at all possible. A festive dish might be chicken cooked in wine ('coq au vin'), or in Burgundy, beef in wine ('bœuf bourgignon'), or in the south a 'bouillabaisse', a Mediterranean fish stew. A popular starter is 'crudités' (page 84) and other courses will include a salad and vegetables which are served separately from the main dish. Bread, fresh from the bakery, is always served with the meal, to mop up the wonderful sauces that are an important part of French cooking.

There is usually some dancing afterwards, often accompanied by a small band or someone playing the accordion, although many young people now prefer a disco.

There is a variety of fine wines to complete any festival. They come from vineyards along the valleys of the Loire, the Garonne and the Rhone. In Brittany and Normandy where grapes do not grow in the cooler climate, cider made from apples is a popular drink and goes well with Breton crêpes.

Famous cheeses such as Brie and Camembert, now common in British shops, are an important part of any meal. They are usually eaten before the dessert, which is likely to be a fruit dish of some kind.

The French eat a light breakfast, usually coffee with crusty French bread (the long stick called a 'baguette') with jam. The main meal of the day is at noon when everything seems to come to a standstill! Even in big cities, supermarkets, banks and shops close, often for up to two hours, but stay open until 7 o'clock in the evening when a light supper is eaten. In the cities this might well be a pizza or a burger: fast food is becoming popular, especially with the young.

Crêpes

These are Breton pancakes. Originally they were made with buckwheat flour and called 'galettes', but nowadays wheat flour is used to make a lighter mixture. The following recipe suggests mixing the two flours, but this is not essential: all plain flour can be used.

75g plain flour	2 medium sized eggs
25g buckwheat flour	30ml melted butter
pinch salt	(or oil)
1 teaspoon sugar	150ml milk and water
(optional – for	clarified butter
sweet fillings)	(or oil or lard) for
	greasing

Sift the flour and salt into a bowl.

Beat the eggs one at a time and stir into the flour with the melted butter or oil.

Stir gently until smooth, gradually adding the milk and water.

Leave to stand in the fridge for 2 hours or more.

Heat a heavy greased frying pan.

Pour in about 3 tablespoons of batter, then swirl around in the pan until the base is covered with a thin layer.

Cook over a medium heat for 1 minute, when bubbles will begin to form underneath.

Shake the pan and carefully turn over with a spatula.

Similarly brown the other side.

Carefully slide onto a heated plate and keep warm while cooking the rest of the batter.

This should make about 12 crêpes.

Fillings

Sweet   jam, honey and lemon juice, grated plain chocolate, cooked, sliced apples or pears

Savoury   grated cheese, fried mushrooms, fried onions, scrambled eggs, finely chopped herbs

Young children can be involved in the preparation and filling of the crêpes, but cooking with hot fat should be done by an adult in charge.

Crudités

Originally from Provence, this is a favourite starter all over France. It consists of a variety of prepared raw vegetables which can be eaten with a vinaigrette dressing or a sauce for dipping into. Ingredients will depend on what is available but vegetables at their prime will be best. Here are some suggestions:

carrots, celery, cucumbers, fennel bulbs, peppers cut into sticks, radishes, broccoli and cauliflower florets, spring onions

Arrange the vegetables attractively on a large plate and garnish with sprigs of watercress, parsley and basil.

Pistou

This is also from Provence. It is a creamy mixture and makes a delicious dip.

5 cloves garlic
1 teaspoon salt
2 handfuls basil leaves
120ml olive oil

50g Gruyère or Parmesan cheese, finely grated
freshly ground black pepper

Crush the garlic and salt with a fork or in a mortar to make a paste.

Mix with the olive oil and basil leaves, in a blender if possible.

Add the grated cheese and pepper and mix thoroughly.

Art and craft

This activity could be linked with the song 'Les sabots de la Duchesse Anne' (page 93). Clogs are seldom worn today, although from time to time clog-type shoes become fashionable. In their day, clogs were the most practical kind of footwear for walking on cobbled streets and pavements.

Pairs of miniature clogs can be fashioned from clay using the method for thumb pots described on page 28 in the section on Greece. Pat the clay into an oblong shape then press out the inside with one thumb, holding the clay in the other

cupped hand. Leave to dry. Reinforced modelling clay will harden on its own. The clogs can then be painted and/or decorated with wild flower designs.

Introduce the children to the music of the Clog Dance from 'La fille mal gardée' by Hérold (1791–1833).

Suggestions for general classroom activities can be found on page 6.

Folk costume

Widely differing costumes throughout the country reflect the individual characteristics of the various regions. But, in general, they are neat and precise with simple bodices, blouses and fairly full skirts. Men's costumes include the loose-fitting worker's smock and styles based on knee breeches, waistcoats, jackets and shirts. A distinctive feature of the costume for both men and women is the headgear. Each region or village will have its own particular design, from neat lace bonnets for women to flat brimmed felt hats for men. 'Sabots' (clogs) were once the main footwear but nowadays ordinary firm shoes are worn. In the south espadrilles or lightweight slippers are popular.

The costumes illustrated in the colour section are from Brittany where there are many occasions such as weddings, local festivals and Sundays when they are worn.

Festivals

Throughout the regions of France the variety of customs, costumes and folk music reflects the mingling of the different peoples that make up today's population.

Regional differences are reflected in the various ways Christmas (Noël) is celebrated. In Alsace and Lorraine and parts of the north, the Christmas tree figures prominently, whereas in Provence it is the 'crèche' with its clay figures called 'santons' that is the main feature.

Religious festivals are important, the majority of the people being Roman Catholic. There are special saints' days, and in Brittany pilgrimages known as 'pardons' are made to the different saints, holy wells and fountains. In Saintes-Maries-de-la-Mer in the Carmargue, gypsies from all over Europe gather twice a year in May and October to honour their patron saint, Sara la Noire (the servant of the three Marys).

In the south and south-west there are special days with bullfights and sports featuring bulls. Many festivals are connected with local industries or crafts, and include wine, flower, fruit and fishing festivals. Flowers play an important part in the festivals. They are carried in processions and used to decorate hoops and baskets. On special occasions they are made into garlands to decorate the fishing boats. On the first day of May (Le Premier Mai) it is customary to give friends and relations a small posy of lilies of the valley.

The major festival is 'le 14 Juillet', France's National Day which commemorates the capture of the Bastille in 1789. This is celebrated in towns and villages all over the country with parades and music and dancing in the streets.

La Marseillaise

'La Marseillaise' was composed in 1792 by an army officer, Rouget de Lisle, a captain of engineers who was also an amateur musician. It was written in response to a request for a marching song after the declaration of war with Austria on 20 April 1792. Troops from Marseille sang it on their march to Paris and it became known as 'La Marseillaise'. In 1795 it was made the national anthem of France by national decree.

English lyrics do not do justice to this fine revolutionary song. The following translation will help the children to understand the French words, but is not intended to be sung:

Come on, children of France!
The day of glory has arrived!
The tyrants have raised
their bloodstained flag against us!
Can you hear their savage soldiers
bellowing in our countryside?
They are coming into our homes
to kill our children and wives.
To arms, citizens!
Form up battalions!
Let's march! Let's march!
Let's water our fields
with their tainted blood!

'La Marseillaise' was written as a marching song, and this is the best way of introducing it. Let the children feel the strong beat and exhilaration of the song by marching to the music on the recording. Start the song with the first two lines and later introduce the last four lines. The children could sing the first two lines and march to the recorded music for the rest of the song if they cannot sing and march at the same time. Encourage them to choreograph a simple pattern of movement.

Suggested accompaniment
Drum or tambour:

Cymbal on the words 'armes' and 'marchons'.

La Marseillaise

Words and music by Rouget de Lisle

In march time

La Carmagnole 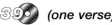 (one verse)

Song of the French Revolution
English words and accompaniment by Jean Gilbert

With rhythm and fervour

(Dance speed ♩. = 120)

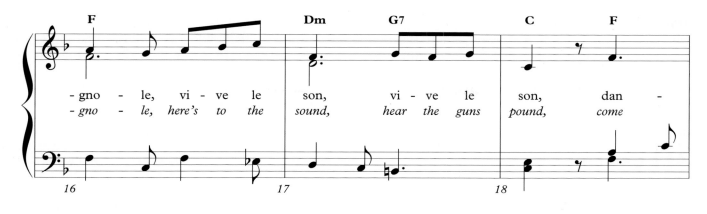

- gno - le, vi - ve le son, vi - ve le son, dan -
- gno - le, here's to the sound, hear the guns pound, come

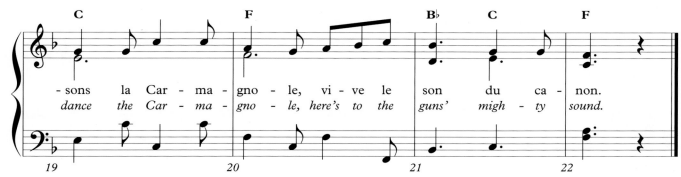

- sons la Car - ma - gno - le, vi - ve le son du ca - non.
dance the Car - ma - gno - le, here's to the guns' migh - ty sound.

2. Monsieur Véto avait promis } *repeat*
d'être fidèle à son pays.
Mais il y a manqué
ne faisons plus quartier.
Dansons la Carmagnole. . .

3. Amis, restons toujours unis, } *repeat*
ne craignons pas nos ennemis.
S'ils vienn'nt nous attaquer
nous les ferons sauter.
Dansons la Carmagnole . . .

2. *Monsieur Véto has made a vow* } *repeat*
he would be true to his country.
His promise did not last,
we'll make him keep it fast.
Come dance the Carmagnole. . .

3. *Remain united all my friends* } *repeat*
and do not fear our enemies.
If ever they attack
then we will gun them back.
Come dance the Carmagnole. . .

This song of the French Revolution ridicules Queen Marie Antoinette ('Madame Véto') and King Louis XVI ('Monsieur Véto') who were both beheaded. The jaunty tune helps to poke fun at the royal couple.

The dance

A simple dance based on figures of the Farandole can be choreographed using a basic step of a skip or a walk.

Here are some suggestions:

Figure 1
bars 1–10 Circle to the right and continue for the repeat.

bars 11–12 4 steps into the centre.

bars 13–14 4 steps back.

bars 15–22 Circle to the left.

Figure 2
bars 1–22 Turn to face partners. Pass partner with right hand and continue round the circle giving alternate hands.

Figure 3
bars 1–22 The circle breaks and a (prearranged) leader leads everyone on a spiral into the centre and out again.

Figure 4

bars 1–22 The circle breaks again. An arch is formed by the end couple and the dancer on the other side of the 'break' leads the line of dancers through the arch and back into a circle.

Start by teaching the first figure and add to this according to the abilities of your group. Figures can be repeated, for example, 1–2–1, to make a simple arrangement. When the children have learnt all the figures, invite them to choreograph their own dance.

Ah! ça ira! 41

Song of the French Revolution
English words by Jean Gilbert

Ah! ça i - ra, ça i - ra, ça i - ra! Les a - ri - sto -
Ah! ça i - ra, ça i - ra, ça i - ra! String up all the

- cra - tes à la lan - ter - ne, Ah! ça i - ra, ça i - ra, ça i -
a - ri - sto - crats se - cure - ly, Ah! ça i - ra, ça i - ra, ça i -

- ra! Les a - ri - sto - cra - tes on les pen - dra!
- ra! All our coun - try's a - ri - sto - crats will hang!

'À la lanterne!' was a phrase used during the Revolution meaning 'string him up!'. 'Ça ira!' means 'we'll manage it!' or 'we'll do it!'

The words given above were sung by students to the song 'Ah! ça ira!' in 1790. These are the words most commonly sung today on 14 July. The song itself is short and easily sung in French. There are no movements but children could make up different patterns of hand-clapping with partners as they sing.

Les gars de Locminé
 (one verse)

The boys of Locminé

Traditional song from Brittany
English words and accompaniment by Jean Gilbert
(Dance speed ♩ = 152)

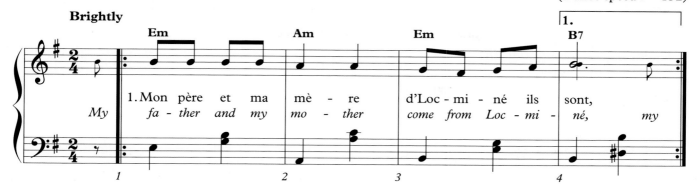

1. Mon père et ma mè - re d'Loc - mi - né ils sont,
My fa - ther and my mo - ther come from Loc - mi - né, my

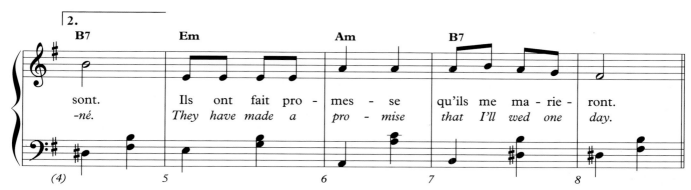

sont. Ils ont fait pro - mes - se qu'ils me ma - rie - ront.
-né. They have made a pro - mise that I'll wed one day.

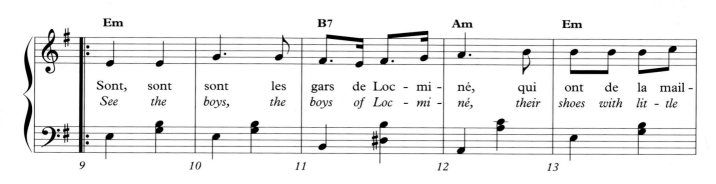

Sont, sont sont les gars de Loc - mi - né, qui ont de la mail -
See the boys, the boys of Loc - mi - né, their shoes with lit - tle

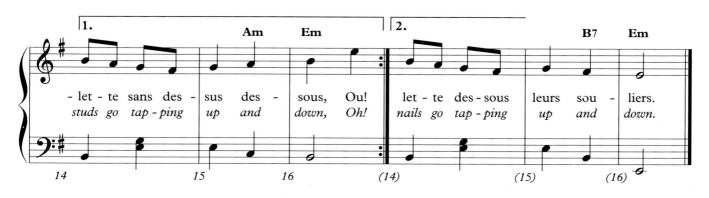

- let - te sans des - sus des - sous, Ou! let - te des - sous leurs sou - liers.
studs go tap - ping up and down, Oh! nails go tap - ping up and down.

91

'Les gars de Locminé' (p.91) and 'Les sabots de la Duchesse Anne' (p.93), both come from Brittany. They are typical of much of the folk music of this beautiful and historic region of France.

Locminé is a small village in the département of Morbihan in south Brittany. The name means 'the place of the monks'.

2. Ils ont fait promesse qu'ils me
      marieront. (*repeat*)
   Nous ferons des crêpes, nous en mangerons.
   Sont, sont, sont . . .

3. Nous ferons des crêpes, nous en mangerons.
      (*repeat*)
   Et si le roi passe, nous lui en ferons.
   Sont, sont, sont . . .

4. Et si le roi passe, nous lui en ferons. (*repeat*)
   Je vendrai mes terres, sillon par sillon.
   Sont, sont, sont . . .

5. Je vendrai mes terres, sillon par sillon. (*repeat*)
   Et sur le dernier bâtirai maison.
   Sont, sont, sont . . .

2. *They have made a promise that I'll wed one
      day. (repeat)*
   *We will make some crêpes and eat them on
      that day.*
   See the boys . . .

3. *We will make some crepes and eat them on
      that day. (repeat)*
   If the king comes by he'll have some on his way.
   See the boys . . .

4. *If the king comes by he'll have some on his
      way. (repeat)*
   I will sell my land, a little day by day.
   See the boys . . .

5. *I will sell my land, a little day by day. (repeat)*
   Build upon the last plot, a house in which to stay.
   See the boys . . .

The dance 43

This is a partner dance performed in a circle. The boys are on the outside facing the girls who have their backs to the centre and their hands on hips.

Figure 1

A	Boys
bars 1–4	Take a side step to the right, close left foot to right foot (2 bars). Step back to the left and close sideways.
bars 1–4	Repeat.
bars 5–3	Repeat to the right only and stamp the right foot.
B	Boys and girls together
bar 9	Tap the right heel in front with the toe pointing up, with a spring on the left foot.
	Spring bringing both feet together.
bar 10	Repeat on the left side.
bars 11–14	Repeat bars 9–10 twice.

bars 15–16	Make a rapid right turn on the spot with arms in the air on the word 'Ou!'.
bars 9–14	Repeat.
bars 15–16	Repeat the turning step on the left side.

Figure 2

A	Girls
bars 1–8	The girls perform the boy's step as given.
B	Boys and girls together
bars 9–16	As before.

Figure 3

A	
bars 1–8	Boys and girls perform as for bars 1–8 starting to the left instead of to the right.
B	
bars 9–16	As before.

Les sabots de la Duchesse Anne

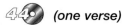 (one verse)

The clogs of the Duchess Anne

15th century French song
English words and accompaniment by Jean Gilbert

In the style of a ballad

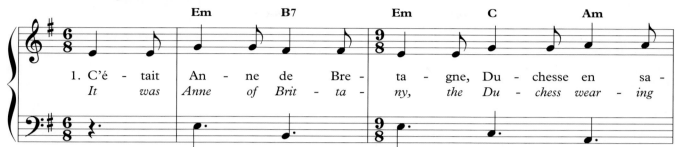

1. C'é - tait An - ne de Bre - ta - gne, Du - chesse en sa -
   It was Anne of Brit - ta - ny, the Du - chess wear - ing

- bots, _____ c'é - tait An - ne de Bre - ta - gne, Du - chesse en sa -
clogs, _____ it was Anne of Brit - ta - ny, the Du - chess wear - ing

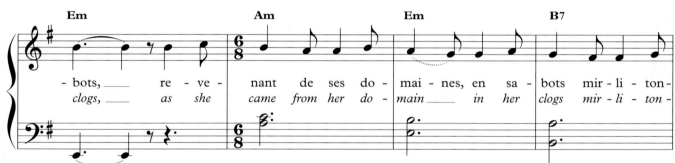

- bots, _____ re - ve - nant de ses do - mai - nes, en sa - bots mir - li - ton -
clogs, _____ as she came from her do - main _____ in her clogs mir - li - ton -

- tai - ne, Ah! Ah! Ah! Vi - vent les sa - bots de bois.
- tai - ne, Ah! Ah! Ah! Won - der - ful clogs made out of wood.

2. Anne de France fut reine, } repeat
   avec des sabots,
   les Bretons sont dans la peine,
   en sabots . . .

3. Ils n'ont plus de souveraine, } repeat
   avec des sabots,
   en France ils suivront leur Reine,
   en sabots . . .

2. *Anne of France was once the queen,* } repeat
   the duchess wearing clogs,
   now the Bretons are in pain,
   in her clogs . . .

3. *They have lost their sovereign queen,* } repeat
   the duchess wearing clogs,
   but in France the Queen is famed,
   in her clogs . . .

* The French word 'mirlitontaine' is derived from 'mirliton' (a toy flute) and has no literal meaning. In the context of the French song it provides a rhythmic ending to the phrase that also rhymes with the previous line. It has not been translated in the English lyrics.

Suggested accompaniment

For the last lines, 'Ah! Ah! Ah! Vivent les sabots de bois!',

claves or woodblocks:

Descant recorders can accompany the tune.

For lists of other resources see page 119.

Duchesse Anne de Bretagne (1477–1514)

When Anne was crowned Duchess as an 11-year-old in Rennes cathedral, Brittany was an independent, autonomous state. She married Charles VIII of France, becoming Queen as well as being Duchess of Brittany before she reached the age of 15. When Charles died, Anne married the new King Louis XII, becoming Queen for the second time. She became the best remembered and most revered ruler of Brittany. When she died at the age of 36, her heart was buried in a golden casket in the cathedral at Nantes. She is referred to, even today, as 'la bonne Duchesse' or 'la petite Brette'.

Sweden

Sverige

Sweden is the largest and most populous of the Scandinavian countries. It is a cold country, especially in the north, where the land actually reaches beyond the Arctic Circle. Snow lies here for eight months. The summers are warm and sunny but very short. The far north is called the 'land of the midnight sun' where, at midsummer, the sun never sets.

Great forests and vast stretches of lakes cover much of central and northern Sweden. From the mountains to the sea, streams and rivers flow through the land. They are home to a rich variety of fish which are caught and cooked with skill and enthusiasm.

Further south, the land is flat and the climate much warmer. Crops, including corn and sugar-beet, are grown here. Rich farmlands provide a wealth of dairy products, fruit and vegetables.

The Swedes are a seafaring people. The availability of wood from the forests, an extended coastline and natural harbours have encouraged a great shipping industry. Wood is exported for building all over the world.

Stockholm, the capital, is built on a group of islands and peninsulas on the east coast. This beautiful city is often called 'the Venice of the North'.

History

The earliest inhabitants of Sweden are said to have been tribes of reindeer hunters who roamed across from the rest of Europe. A German tribe called the Svear settled in the area near Lake Mälaren around AD 98 and gave their name to the whole country. Central and southern Sweden was later conquered by tribes coming mostly from Norway and Denmark. These were the Vikings, strong, seafaring people who went on to invade other parts of Europe and North America.

Towards the end of the Viking age several small Swedish states were united into one kingdom and many Swedes had converted to Christianity. King Olaf Eriksson was baptized in about 1008. By the middle of the twelfth century the country was united enough to begin the conquest of Finland.

In 1397 Sweden and Norway came under the rule of Denmark. This was very unpopular with the Swedes who made attempts to break away. Finally Gustav Vasa, a young Swedish nobleman, gathered together an army and drove the Danes out of the country. He was made King in 1523 and under his rule Sweden became strong and independent.

Sweden remained a powerful country, although in 1809 the Swedes were forced to give up Finland to Russia. After a short war in 1814, Sweden formed a union with Norway. The union was ended peacefully in 1905.

Today Sweden is an independent democratic state which has kept out of all wars since 1814. It remained neutral during the last two world wars. Partly because of this it has provided a home for immigrants from other European countries and for political refugees from all over the world.

Some famous people

Literature

August Strindberg (1849–1912) is considered the greatest writer of modern Sweden. His work includes novels, plays and historical dramas.

Science

Anders Celsius (1701–44) invented and gave his name to the 100-degree thermometer.

Carolus Linnaeus (1707–78) worked out a system for classifying plants and animals.

Carl Scheele (1742–86) made many chemical discoveries. He showed that air consisted chiefly of oxygen and nitrogen.

Alfred Nobel (1833–96) was the inventor of dynamite and established a number of international prizes which bear his name.

Music

Swedish musicians include two internationally famous opera singers, **Jenny Lind** (1820–87) and **Birgit Nilsson** (1922–).

Film

Greta Garbo (1905–90) and **Ingrid Bergman** (1915–82) were both well-known film-stars. Their films are still shown all over the world.

Ingmar Bergman (1918-), film and stage director, has a worldwide reputation for his many beautiful and haunting films.

Main crops:

dairy products, meat, cereals, potatoes, timber

People's jobs:

Agricultural 4%
Industrial 25%
Other 71%

Main industries:

transport equipment, foodstuffs, paper, machinery, metal products, wood products, chemicals, electrical goods

Language

Swedish belongs to the North Germanic or Scandinavian language group.

English	Swedish
one	en
two	två
three	tre
four	fyra
five	fem
six	sex
seven	sju
eight	åtta
nine	nio
ten	tio
good morning	god morgon
good afternoon	god middag
good evening	god kväll
hello!	hej!
how are things?	hur är det?
fine	bra
thank you	tack
please	var så god
yes	ja
no	nej
goodbye	hejdå

Suggestions for language activities can be found on page 7.

Food and drink

Today in Sweden meals are planned to suit modern living. It is common for both husband and wife to work, so the main meal of the day is in the evening between 5 and 7 pm. It is usually a main dish of meat or fish with potatoes and perhaps fruit and a piece of cheese for dessert. With an early start to the day, breakfast means coffee or tea with bread, butter and cheese or cereals with milk or yoghurt. Lunch in a canteen or quick-service restaurant is a light meal with one hot dish and usually a glass of milk. Traditionally the Swedes drink coffee either black or with cream.

For weekends and holiday times a favourite spread is the famous 'smörgåsbord', which is a delicious buffet meal. A long table is set with attractively prepared dishes, and guests help themselves. There will be a variety of herring dishes (served with steaming boiled potatoes, thick sour cream, chopped chives and sliced onions), also salmon, eel and shrimps. Additional dishes will include cold meats such as smoked reindeer meat and a good choice of cheeses and salads. At home the smörgåsbord will consist of a few family favourites.

In between times there is a 'smörgås' for any occasion: morning coffee, a quick lunch or the odd snack. This will be an open sandwich, just a slice of bread and butter topped with a slice of cheese or sausage or whatever is available.

During the summer months the Swedes love to eat tender young vegetables and fresh soft fruit, strawberries, raspberries, blueberries and cloudberries.

Midsummer ('Midsommar') is one of the bigger traditional festivals in Sweden. This is not surprising in a land where the winter is long and summer is short but intense. Homes, churches and streets are decorated with garlands of flowers and leafy branches and the day is spent singing, dancing and feasting. The traditional lunch on Midsummer's Day will include different kinds of pickled herring served with new potatoes boiled with dill, fermented cream and chopped chives followed by fresh strawberries.

Hannas äppelkaka (Hanna's apple cake)

$\frac{3}{4}$ cup ground blanched almonds

100g butter

6 tablespoons sugar

2 egg yolks

3 egg whites

juice and grated rind of $\frac{1}{2}$ lemon

6–8 apples, pre-cooked with sugar, or raw and thinly sliced

Place the well-drained apples in a shallow, buttered baking dish.

Cream the butter and sugar until light and fluffy.

Gradually blend in the egg yolks, ground almonds, lemon rind and juice.

Beat the egg whites and carefully fold into the almond batter.

Spread over the apples and bake for 15 minutes in a preheated oven at gas mark 6, 400° F (200°C) until golden.

Serves 5–6.

Matjessill (Sweet-pickled herring)

This is the most important dish on the Swedish smörgåsbord and the easiest to prepare.

200g sweet-pickled
  herring
4 tablespoons
  chopped chives
$\frac{3}{4}$ cup sour cream
1 red onion, sliced
  in rings
fresh dill sprigs
$\frac{1}{2}$ kg unpeeled potatoes,
  preferably small, new ones

Cut the herring fillets on the diagonal into 2cm pieces.

Arrange on a serving dish and garnish with fresh dill and onion rings.

Serve sour cream and chives either mixed together or in separate dishes.

A bowl of steaming potatoes together with rye crisp bread, butter and a hard cheese will complete a first course dish.

For another culinary occasion, organize a simple smörgåsbord or make some smörgås for lunch one day. Include a dish of matjessill and some äpplekaka.

Art and craft

Handicraft and domestic industry have very old traditions in Sweden. Beautiful articles such as patterned woollen sweaters, baskets and wrought-iron candelabra are still made.

Dalecarlia (Dalarna) is famous for its painted wooden horses which have been made since 1840. Originally intended as toys or ornaments for the home, they are now exported all over the world. The wood for the horses comes from the forests around the Dalecarlian lakes, where the trees grow very slowly and produce strong wood which is easily treated. Most of the horses are made of pine wood but the smallest are made of alder. Once the horses are carved they are painted red, blue or black with manes and saddles of many colours.

The outline below could be transferred to strong paper or card and painted or coloured by the children.

Suggestions for general classroom activities can be found on page 6.

Folk costume

Costumes are fairly simple in style and usually made from homespun materials. Each region has its own type of apron, which can be plain with stripes or flowered or checked. In place of pockets, flat bags embroidered with bright coloured wools are suspended from the waistband. Shawls are usually worn as capes, and a small bonnet or cap completes the costume. It was customary for married women to tuck their hair well out of sight.

The illustrated costumes in the colour section come from Rättvik in Dalecarlia. The woman wears a neckerchief rather than a shawl and her striped apron is in fact part of the skirt. The man's hat has dangling red pompoms indicating that he is a bachelor; a married man would have black pompoms!

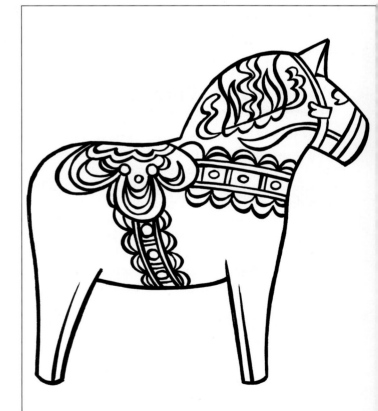

A wooden horse

Festivals

After the long dark winter of the north, Sweden welcomes the return of spring and summer. Large bonfires are lit on Walpurgis Night ('Valborgsmässoafton', on 30 April) and parties are held to 'sing in the spring'. But the most popular festival is that of Midsummer ('Midsommar') when summer is only just beginning. This is celebrated on the weekend nearest to 24 June, the feast day of Saint John, and in many respects resembles May Day festivities.

Celebrations begin on the morning of Midsummer Eve when Swedes decorate their homes, cars, churches and meeting places with garlands of flowers and leafy branches. In the afternoon the 'majstång' (maypole) is raised in the centre of the village square or local community, the fiddlers strike up and the dancing begins.

As with many other 'eves', Midsummer Eve was believed to be a night of supernatural happenings and magical powers. Midsummer dew and certain young plants were thought to cure illnesses. A favourite custom of young girls was to place a bouquet of nine different flowers under their pillows to help them dream of their future husbands. The ancient custom of lighting fires at Midsummer in honour of the sun still continues here and in many other places across Europe.

The festival celebrating the 'Queen of Light' comes just before Christmas on 13 December when, according to folk tradition, the nights are at their longest. This is Lucia Day ('Luciadagen') when the eldest girl of a family, dressed in white and wearing a crown of lighted candles, offers coffee and saffron buns to everyone in the house.

The following dance songs are typical of many that are sung and danced during the festival of Midsommar.

Jungfru, jungfru

The dance

The children dance in a ring in either of the following formations:

The boys form a middle ring, holding hands and facing inwards. The girls stand behind with hands on their partner's shoulders or waist.

or

Boys and girls stand alternately in a ring, hands linked behind.

bars 1–8 Light springs on alternate feet on the spot, feet kicking forward.

bars 9–12 Side gallop to the left.

bars 9–12 Side gallop to the right. Feet come
(repeat) together on the last word 'ja'.

Suggested accompaniment

bar 5 tambourine on the word 'tio' (ten)
bar 6 triangle on the word 'fem' (five)

bars 7–8: tambourine shake getting louder towards the chorus

Chorus: tambourine throughout

Jungfru, jungfru

Maiden, maiden

Traditional song
English words by Jean Gilbert

Känner du Lotta, min vän

Do you know Lotta my friend

Traditional song
English words by Jean Gilbert

Suggested accompaniment

bars 2–8: triangle

$$\frac{3}{4}\ \; \text{𝅗𝅥.} \quad | \quad \text{𝅗𝅥.} \quad :||$$

bars 9–16: tambourine

$$\frac{3}{4}\ \; \text{♩ ♩ ♩} \quad | \quad \text{♩ ♩ ♩} \quad :||$$

The dance 49

This is a dance for couples which can be done either in a circle or in pairs. The children face one another standing side by side. They hold hands with left elbows bent and right arms extended.

Introduction (bar 1)	3 slow claps, then take hands using the hold as described.
bars 2–8	Children circle round in their own space going forward with small walking steps.
bars 9–16	Children circle backwards with small steps.

Repeat the dance changing sides with the right elbow bent and the left arm extended.

Flickorna de små uti ringen de gå 50

The little girls walk in a circle

Traditional song
English words by Jean Gilbert

March time

(Dance speed ♩ = 120)

Flick - or - na de små u - ti ring - en de gå, de
See the lit - tle girls as they cir - cle a - round, and

tänk - a just som så en vän jag kund - e få, och
this is what they say, if you will be my friend, and

om du vill bli all - ra kä - ras - ten min, så
if you will be my own part - ner for once, oh

Suggested accompaniment

bars 17–32: tambourine

The dance

Divide the children equally into two concentric circles.

bars 1–8 Promenade (walk) going in different directions in the circle. Holding hands might help younger children to keep the shape of the circle.

bars 9–14 Children face the partner they come to, take hands and promenade clockwise with their partner in a circle.

bars 15–16 Face partner and take a 'waltz' hold.

bars 17–24 Sideways gallop, continuing clockwise.

bars 25–32 Take hands again to promenade with partners as for bars 9–14. *Repeat bars 17–32.*

The dance can be continued from the beginning with different partners, dancing anticlockwise.

The dance could be simplified for younger children:

bars 1–8 Children walk or skip round in a single circle, hands joined.

bars 9–16 Change direction.

bars 17–24 Side gallop, direction optional.

bars 25–32 Walk round, direction optional.

The children could try making up their own dance to this tune, with a partner or in a small circle.

Notes on steps

'Promenade' means to walk in time with the music with an easy movement but good body stance. When promenading with a partner, inside hands can be joined or both hands joined crosswise and held high in front at shoulder level.

'Side gallop' is merely a sideways version of a forward gallop. Going to the right, step on to right foot. Bring left foot across and hop, shooting right foot out to the right for the next gallop.

For lists of other resources see page 120.

May Day

May Day celebrates the joy of spring. It welcomes the return of longer, warmer days after the harshness of the winter months. Throughout Europe it is a time of looking forward, a time when trees blossom, wild flowers grow in profusion and green shoots heralding the summer harvest colour the fields.

The origins of May Day celebrations are very old. Some people believe that they began with the tree worship of the old Druid religion. We know that the Romans had a spring festival, 'Floralia', when they gathered spring flowers to honour Flora, the goddess of fruit and flowers. It is thought that this could be the origin of May Day in countries that were occupied or influenced by the Romans at the time of the Roman Empire.

The Celtic peoples of Europe celebrated the start of summer with a festival called 'Beltane', meaning 'bright fire', when bonfires were lit on the eve of May Day. In Britain, place names like Tullybelton ('Beltane Hill') and Tan-y-bryn ('fire-hill') recall this ancient festival. A Beltane Fair is still held in Peebles at this time of year.

In Italy young Italians would bring blossoming branches to relatives and friends to decorate front doors and bring colour to the streets. In Greece, young people still use the May Day holiday for making excursions into the countryside. They bring back flowers to decorate doorways and balconies. In France, lily-of-the-valley are exchanged to bring good luck to friends. A sprig of 'lucky' heather may sometimes be given in Britain.

May Day was also a time for courting when young men and women began to think of marriage. German boys would secretly plant young May trees below the windows of their girl friends, whilst Czech boys would place a maypole instead. In Switzerland the 'Maitannli', the May pine, was decorated and set before the young lady's window. Teachers in Lorraine in France were also favoured in this way. In rural areas some of these customs still survive.

May Day in Britain

Long ago in Britain, May Day was the major festival of the year. Throughout the country people gathered flowers and greenery from the woods to decorate their houses, a custom known as 'bringing in the May' and they celebrated the first of May with music, dancing round a maypole, games and feasting.

During the Middle Ages, Morris dancing, sports and simple plays became popular. These May Games, as they were known, were presided over by a May Queen or May Lady and a May King. Robin Hood was a popular character associated with May Day. He was often the hero of May Day plays and someone dressed up as him might be seen among the May Day revellers. Sometimes a mystical figure dressed in green and covered in leaves and branches would take part in processions. He was described as 'Jack-in-the-Green', but is generally referred to as 'the Green Man'. Like other characters he was a symbol of spring. May fairs were also held in some towns and villages. In London they were held in the district called Mayfair!

The Puritans discouraged the revelry of 'maying' and their parliament banned all maypoles. When Charles II was restored to the throne the ban was

Morris dancers

The Padstow Hobby Horse

The procession of the 'Obby Oss' at Padstow in Cornwall is probably the most important real surviving tradition of May Day. The rites are very, very old. A similar horse appears in several English seasonal folk events that seem to have origins in fertility ritual.

Every May Day thousands of people visit Padstow to see the two famous Hobby Horses, the 'Blue Ribbon' or 'Peace Oss' and the 'Old Oss'.

Each 'Oss' is portrayed by a man covered by a long-skirted black tarpaulin which billows over a six-foot hoop swung from his shoulders. Over his face he wears a fearsome mask, part horse, part dragon, topped by a tall pointed hat.

Driven by a Teaser, he dances his way through the streets with curious twisting and diving movements to the accompaniment of accordion, drums and singing. He occasionally charges into the crowd to corner a young girl and to pinch her. This is believed to bring her luck in the form of a husband or baby within the year.

lifted and some of the old customs gradually returned.

May Day became popular again in the mid-nineteenth century, but the festival revived by the Victorians was really only a prettified version of some of the old customs.

Today there are still many May Day celebrations. Morris men dance at dawn in a number of places. In Oxford and Southampton, choristers sing on May Morning. At Knutsford in Cheshire, the May Queen, together with all the traditional characters and teams of Morris dancers, takes part in a modern revival of the May Games.

There are a few surviving ceremonies that are rooted in the more ancient traditions. Among these are the Padstow Hobby Horse and the Helston Furry Dance, described in the following sections.

Sometimes the 'Oss will sink to the ground as if dying while the slower part of the song (verse 6) is sung: 'Oh, where is St George, oh, where is he, oh?'. The 'Oss is then coaxed back to life by the Teaser and any young children who pluck up courage to come and touch him. He is soon up again as the drummers madly beat their drums, and continues his curious dance to the first lively tune (verse 7): 'with the merry ring, adieu the merry spring'. The procession is led by a band of young men in white with blue or red ribbons and a 'drum major' who conducts the music to accompany the dance of the 'Oss.

The 'Obby Oss' being teased

The Padstow May-day song

 *(verses 1, 2, 6)*

Traditional song
Accompaniment adapted by Jean Gilbert

107

2. Arise up Mr ——, I know you well afine,
   for summer . . .

   You have a shilling in your purse and I wish it
   was in mine, *in the merry* . . .

3. Arise up Miss ——, all in your gown of
   green . . .

   You are as fine a lady as wait upon the
   Queen . . .

4. The young men of Padstow they might if they
   would . . .

   They might have built a ship and gilded her
   with gold . . .

5. The young women of Padstow they might if
   they would . . .

   They might have made a garland with the white
   rose and the red . . .

6. Oh, where is St George . . . (see slow tune)

7. With the merry ring, adieu the merry spring ...

How happy is the little bird that merrily doth
sing . . .

8. Now fare you well and bid you all good
   cheer . . .

   We call no more unto your house before
   another year . . .

   * Aunt Ursula Birdwood is unknown.
   † 'yow' = 'ewe'.

Many different versions of the verses can be
found. The children could improvise their own
verses based on people they know.

Suggested accompaniment

Traditionally the song is accompanied by drums
and accordions. The Padstow 'sound' could be
improvised with deep tambours and a harmonium
or melodicas, the tambour playing on the beat
and the melody instruments playing the tune.
Other instruments could join in or play on their
own, the descant and/or tenor recorder, for
example.

The Helston Furry Dance

The Helston Furry Dance, which takes place on 8 May (or the previous Saturday if 8 May falls on a Sunday), is part of one of the most famous of surviving British traditional festivals. It is known locally as 'the Furry' but also as 'Floral' or 'Flora Day', names associated with the Roman goddess Flora. The word 'furry' has various probable derivations: the Cornish 'fer' (Latin 'feria') for holy or feast day, 'ferrie', the English word implying a church festival and 'fairie', meaning market or fair.

The dance which is performed in the streets of Helston, is said to be a survival of an ancient pagan ritual dance. The seasonal setting suggests that it is essentially a spring festival, the dance being an expression of joy at the triumph of Life (spring) over Death (winter). According to legend, the first furry was danced to celebrate the victory of St Michael, the patron saint of Helston, over the Devil for the possession of Helston. During the battle a mighty stone was thrown and landed near the Angel Inn. Part of the 'Hell's Stone', a name said to be associated with that of the town, may still be visible embedded in a wall nearby.

The festival includes a maying procession called the 'Hal-an-Tow', linking it with the celebrations of May Day. This takes place in the morning on Furry Day when all the characters mentioned in the verses, as well as St Michael, lead the procession through the narrow streets of the town, stopping at intervals to sing the song.

The Helston Furry dance

Traditional tune
Accompaniment adapted by Jean Gilbert

* as many times as required

The Furry or Floral dance is performed at various times during the day but the main dance is at noon. This is led by the mayor and was originally for the gentry of the town, the dress code being long dresses and summer hats for ladies and grey toppers and morning coats for their partners. The couples dance their way through the narrow, decorated streets, weaving through any houses or gardens left open to them, for it was believed that this would bring good luck to the household. The last dance is open to any spectators who wish to join in.

The dance

This is performed in a long line of couples and can be described as a very simple processional morris dance.

Dancers number off in groups of two couples, ladies standing to the right of their partners. The dance is in two parts:

A music Dancers process on using a jaunty walking step. The man leads his partner by the right hand.

B music Men change places and turn their opposite partners with both hands. They change back again and turn their own partners.

The dance proceeds in this way, the tune being repeated as many times as may be required.

Suggested accompaniment

Traditionally the dance is accompanied by the Helston town band. A suitable accompaniment is provided on the CD which comes with this book. However, the melody could be played by instruments such as recorder, melodica or accordion. A good drum or deep-sounding tambour could mark the beat and keep the time steady.

Dress

The children of Helston dress all in white for the Children's Dance. Girls wear distinctive garlands according to their school and the boys wear lily-of-the-valley buttonholes pinned to their shirts. This is the special flower for May Day.

The Hal-an-tow *(one verse)*

Traditional song
Accompaniment by Jean Gilbert

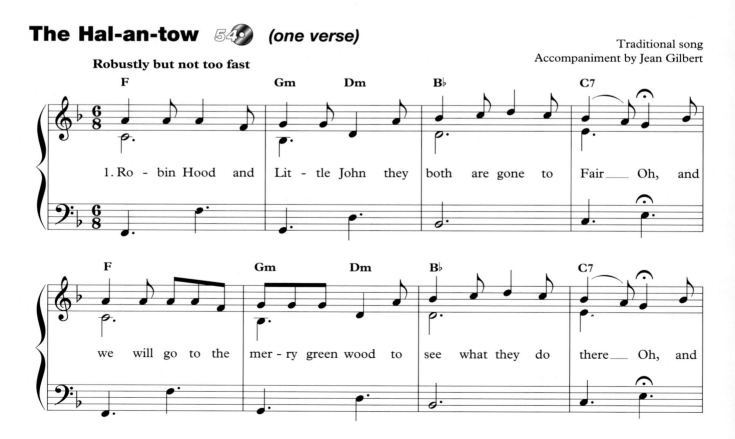

2. Where are those Spaniards
   that make so great a boast, Oh?
   They shall eat the grey goose feather
   and we will eat the roast, Oh,
   in every land, Oh,
   the land where'er we go.

   Hal-an-tow . . .

3. As for that good knight St George,
   St George he was a knight, Oh!
   Of all the knights in Christendom
   St George he is the right, Oh,
   in every land, Oh,
   the land where'er we go.

   Hal-an-tow . . .

4. But to a greater than St George,
   our Helston has a right, Oh,
   St Michael with his wings outspread,
   the Archangel so bright, Oh,
   who fought the fiend, Oh,
   of all mankind the foe!

   Hal-an-tow . . .

The name 'Hal-an-tow' is said to be of Flemish or Dutch origin. 'Haal aan het touw' means 'heave on the rope'. However it has also been thought to refer to the 'heel and toe' dance which is still danced in the English Cotswold morris tradition.

The last verse was added in modern times.

To 'rumble' is to move or stir actively.

'Spaniards' may refer to the Armada.

Ribbon dance 55

Traditional tune
Accompaniment by Jean Gilbert

The use of ribbons in this simple country dance makes it a particularly attractive one for a May Day celebration.

The children are grouped into longways sets for 6 couples. Each couple holds a ribbon or sash (about 1 metre in length) between them in their right hands.

A The 1st, 3rd and 5th couples move down a place holding up their ribbons as arches under which the 2nd, 4th and 6th couples pass to move up a place. This process is reversed, returning couples to their places.

The whole movement is then repeated.

B1 The 6th couple remains in position making an arch with their ribbons. The other couples face front and follow the first couple who 'cast' or skip away from one another and dance round to meet each other going under the arch and returning to their places.

Each girl on separating from her partner tosses the end of her ribbon over to him. He receives it and gives it back to her when they meet to pass under the arch.

B2 The first couple join hands and swing down the middle under the arches made by the other couples, to become the last couple.

The dance continues with couples in different places.

The final (sixth) round

B1 and B2 After the 'cast' the leading couple reaches the bottom to pass under the arch, but instead of dancing to the top of the set, they make an arch immediately next to the bottom one. The next couple passes under the two arches to make a third arch and so on until all the arches have been built.

At the end the girls throw their end of the ribbon high into the air across to the boys and partners bow.

Steps

Dancers should use a lilting walk in the arches and a skipping step in the cast-and-swing.

Good-morning, lords and ladies

(Not included on the CD)

Traditional song
Accompaniment by Jean Gilbert

Simply

1. Good morn - ing lords and la - dies, it is the first of May. Come

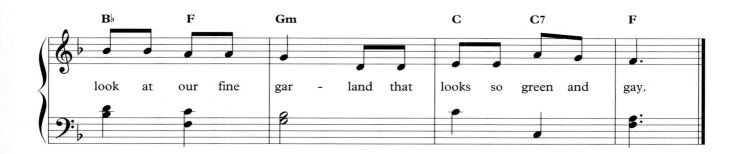

look at our fine gar - land that looks so green and gay.

May Day activities

Songs

'Good-morning, lords and ladies' (page 113), is from Cottesmore in Rutland, collected by Elizabeth Ruddock. There are three more verses:

2. The cuckoo sings in April,
   the cuckoo sings in May,
   the cuckoo sings in June, July,
   and then she flies away.

3. I have a bag lies on my arm,
   'tis lined with silk and string,
   and all we want is a silver piece
   to line it well within.

4. Good-morning all, both great and small,
   we wish you a joyful day.
   Good-morning all both great and small,
   we wish you all good-day.

Introduce some more May Day songs, here are some to choose from:

'Now is the month of maying', 'Come, lasses and lads', 'To the maypole haste' from *The New National Song Book* (Boosey and Hawkes, 1958)

'Bromham May song' and 'May garlands' from *A Musical Calendar of Festivals* by Barbara Cass-Beggs (Ward Lock Educational, 1983)

'May Morn' from *The Song-Tree* by Gordon Hitchcock (Curwen, 1965)

Country dancing

Country dancing is a natural development of the singing game. Activities for younger children could include old favourites such as 'Looby Loo', 'Shoo fly' and 'Round and round the village'. For more country dances to go with the 'Ribbon dance' a booklet and cassette for primary schools, *Country Dancing,* is published by Scholastic Publications Ltd. The English Folk Dance and Song Society's Folk Shop catalogue has a wide range of resource materials (see 'Useful addresses', p. 120).

Maypole dancing

Maypole dancing is exciting to watch and fun to do but requires precision, control and a lot of practice. The following publications give a sound introduction:

Maypole Dances, W. Shaw (Curwen, 1954)
Maypole Dances, Sandy Mason (Sandy Mason, 1988)

Both are available through the English Folk Dance and Song Society (see 'Useful addresses', p. 120).

General activities

● Build a frieze around the classroom to include the various May Day activities that have been introduced to the children. This could be an historical survey starting with the ancient Beltane festival, a typical May Day scene from the Middle Ages or a May fair.

● Make a bonfire collage from coloured tissue and silver foil mounted on dark card, or use this idea to create a 3D effect on the frieze.

● Make a Green Man or a Green Man costume. For the costume a base could be made from a tube of green cloth with a hoop inside to make it move and sway. Alternatively make a simple tunic from green cloth. Decorate with leafy twigs and/or leafy fabric. A headcovering could be improvised from a green beret suitably decorated, or leaves and twigs could be entwined or clipped into the hair.

● Visit a local park or woody area and learn to identify trees, particularly 'Maypole' trees such as birch, ash, elm, larch and pine. Collect their leaves to make drawings or prints which could also be used on the frieze.

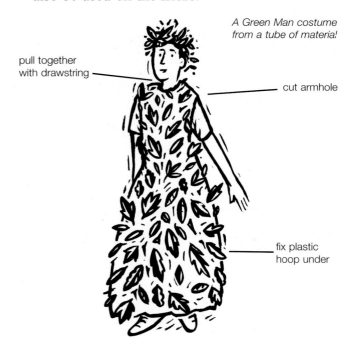

A Green Man costume from a tube of material

pull together with drawstring

cut armhole

fix plastic hoop under

● Make a Victoria sandwich cake:

Victoria sandwich cake

175g butter
175g castor sugar
3 large eggs
175g self-raising flour

Cream the butter and sugar until smooth and creamy.

Add the well-beaten eggs, one at a time.

Sieve the flour and fold into the mixture.

Divide between two greased sandwich tins (15–18 cm).

Bake in a moderate oven, gas mark 4, 350°F (180°C) for 20 minutes. When cooked the cake should be pale golden in colour and shrinking away from the edge of the tins.

Turn out to cool on a wire rack.

When completely cold, sandwich together with a layer of strawberry jam and a little whipped double cream.

Improvise a maypole decoration on the top. A butter icing, coloured green for grass, could support a maypole of barley sugar pushed into the centre. 'Ribbons' of coloured cotton or thin wool could be fixed to jelly babies set at intervals around the edges.

● Make some May garlands. Real leaves and flowers have a limited life unless treated, but look beautiful. Otherwise, use coloured tissue or artificial flowers if available. Attach them to sticks and hang some ribbons from the top. Alternatively, cover two hoops with flowers and ribbons, put one inside the other at right angles and suspend a small doll from the middle. A bigger garland could be made from three circles of wire and a fairly straight, strong stick. Attach the wire circles with nails to the stick, the smallest at the top. Bind with coloured paper or streamers and decorate with flowers, leaves and grasses. A cane basket can also be filled and decorated.

● Organize a May Festival. This could include a May crowning ceremony, a garland competition, country dancing, dancing round a maypole and May games — all the fun of the fair! More ambitious ideas could include dressing up in medieval costume, even inviting a guest Morris dance team.

For lists of other resources see page 120.

Resources

The details contained in this section are correct at the time of going to print. The lists of books and recorded music are not fully comprehensive but are intended to give some idea of the range of material available. Titles may be withdrawn or replaced from time to time. In the case of recorded music, current lists can be obtained from the distributors or record shops:

ARC Music Distribution (UK) Ltd, PO Box 111, East Grinstead, West Sussex RH19 4FZ (tel: 01342 312161)

Discovery Records, The Old Church Mission Room, 5 Kings Corner, Pewsey, Wiltshire SN9 5BS (tel: 01672 563931)

Harmonia Mundi, 19 Nile Street, London N1 7LL (tel: 0171 253 0863)

Koch International Ltd, 24 Concord Road, London W3 0TH (tel: 0181 992 7177)

Rykodisc Ltd, 78 Stanley Gardens, London W3 7SZ (tel: 0181 746 1234)

Topic Records and Direct Distribution, 50 Stroud Green Road, London N4 3EF (tel: 0171 263 1214 and 0171 281 3465)

HMV UK Ltd, 150 Oxford Street, London W1N 0DJ (tel: 0171 201 5430)

Tower Records, 1 Piccadilly Circus, London W1R 8TR (tel: 0171 439 2500)

General reference

Reference books

A Celebration of Customs and Rituals of the World, Robert Ingpen and Philip Wilkinson (Dragon's World, 1994)

Aspects of Folk Dance in Europe, Helen Wingrave and Robert Harrold (Dance Books, 1984)

Dancing into Europe (Society for International Folk Dancing, 1993). A selection of folk dances from countries of the E.U. suitable for use with children in primary schools, together with information on costumes and customs designed to encourage research into the traditions of these countries. Booklet and cassette available from Mrs Eleanor Gordon, 92 Norbiton Avenue, Kingston-upon-Thames, Surrey KT1 3QP.
The S.I.F.D. runs day and residential courses for adults in different parts of the country.

Festival Europe: Fairs and Celebrations throughout Europe, Margaret M Johnson (Mustang Publishing Company, 1992)

Folk Costumes of the World, Robert Harrold and Phyllida Legg (Blandford, 1978)

World Music: The Rough Guide (The Rough Guides, 1994). This comprehensive handbook describes the music of the various countries or regions and provides a selective discography for each section.

Children's books

Europe's History, Deborah Elliott (Wayland, 1994)

The History of Europe, Brian Dicks (Wayland, 1994)

The Usborne Book of Europe: A history of its culture, politics and people, Rebecca Treays (Usborne, 1993)

Additional resources

European Community Folk Culture on CD-ROM from Edinburgh Multimedia, 3 Hayfield, Edinburgh EH12 8UJ Scotland (tel: 0131 339 5374). Includes music sheets, songs, dance descriptions, video clips, dress images, festival contacts, quizzes. Covers Belgium, Denmark, England, France, Germany, Greece, Ireland, Italy, Netherlands, Portugal, Scotland and Spain.

The British Library National Sound Archive, 29 Exhibition Road, London SW7 2AS, is one of the largest sound archives in the world. The international music curator (tel: 0171-412 7427) provides an information resource centre for teachers who require specific advice regarding the selection of and access to suitable sound recordings.

Spain

Book list

A Taste of Spain, B. Goodwin and C. Perez (Wayland, 1994)

Focus on Spain and the Spanish, Ed Needham (Watts, 1993)

Getting to know Spain and Spanish, Janet de Saulles (Watts, 1993)

Look Inside Spain, Ian James and Joy Richardson (Watts, 1995)

Passport to Spain, Keith Lye (Watts, 1992)

Spain (from the 'Our Country' series), David Cumming (Wayland, 1991)

Spain: Country Fact Files, Anna Selby (Wayland, 1993)

First 1000 Words in Spanish, H. Amery (Usborne, 1995)

500 Really Useful Spanish Words and Phrases, Carol Watson and Janet de Saulles (Watts, 1993)

Spanish for Beginners (tape pack), A. Wilkes (Usborne, 1992)

Recorded music

Cobles Catalan: The history of Catalan music, AUVIDIS/SILEX Y 225102, and other recordings (distributed by Harmonia Mundi)

La Musgana: Traditional music from Spain, Green Linnet GLCD 4010, (distributed by Topic)

ARC Music has a number of listings of flamenco including:

Flamenco: Los Alhama, EU/MC/CD 1026

Best of Flamenco, EU/MC/CD 1158

Classical music:

Albeniz: Iberia Suite

Granados: 12 Danzas Espagnolas

Falla: Nights in the Gardens of Spain

The following works are by French composers but are inspired by Spain:

Bizet: 'Toreador's Song' from Carmen

Ravel: Boléro and Rapsodie espagñole

Chabrier: España — Jota

Useful addresses

The Spanish Embassy (Education Office), 20 Peel Street, London W8 7PD (tel: 0171-727 2462)

The Cervantes Institute, 22 Manchester Square, London W1M 5AP (tel: 0171-486 4350)

Greece

Book list

Ancient Greece: Everyday Life, A. Millard (Usborne Publishing, 1994)

Ancient Greece, Bev Knott and Tim Franks (OUP, 1994)

Ancient Greece (from the 'See Through History' series), Rowena Loverance (Heinemann, 1992)

Greece (from the 'Countries of the World' series), Peggy Hollinger (Wayland, 1994)

Greece (from the 'Our Country' series), Julia Waterlow (Wayland, 1991)

Greek Myths and Legends, C. Evans and A. Millard (Usborne, 1994)

The Ancient Greeks (from the 'Our World: History' series), Pat Taylor (Heinemann, 1992)

The Greeks (from the 'Understanding People in the Past' series), Rosemary Rees (Heinemann, 1994)

The Greeks (from the 'Look into the Past' series), Susan Williams (Wayland, 1993)

Recorded music

The biggest stockist of Greek music in the UK is the Trehantiri Record Shop (see 'Useful addresses'). Their listings include:

Folk and Island Music from All Regions, Lyra 4667/68

Viva Bouzouki, FM MYTHOS 600

'Zorba the Greek' and other hits, FM MYTHOS 605

ARC Music has a number of listings including:

The Athenians: Best of Greece Vol 11, EU/MC/CD 1159 (songs and folk tunes in different musical styles)

Romiosini: Songs and Dances from Greece, EUMC/CD 1163

Michalis Terzis: Orchesteca, EUCD/MC 1206 (instruments include the bouzouki, sanduri, baglama, accordion and guitar)

Useful addresses

Embassy of Greece, 1a Holland Park, London W11 3TP (tel: 0171-221 6467)

The Greek National Tourist Organisation, 4 Conduit Street, London W1R 0DJ (tel: 0171-734 5997)

The Hellenic Centre, 16–18 Paddington Street, London W1M 4AS (tel: 0171-487 5060)

Zeno (The Greek Bookshop), 6 Denmark Street, London WC2H 8LP (tel: 0171-836 2522)

Hellenic Bookservice, 91 Fortess Road, London NW5 1AG (tel: 0171-267 9499)

Trehantiri Record Shop, 367 Green Lanes, London N4 1DY (tel: 0181-802 6530)

Bulgaria

Book list

Dances, Music and Costumes of Bulgaria, Helen Wingrave and Robert Harrold (1978), available from Dance Books Ltd, 9, Cecil Court, London WC2N 4EZ

There is very little material suitable for classroom use, but many of the travel guides such as *Bulgaria: The Rough Guide* held in most public libraries have good illustrations and interesting notes. Illustrated brochures can also be obtained from Balkan Holidays London (see 'Useful addresses').

Recorded music

Music of Bulgaria, Hannibal Records HNBC (HNCD) 1335, and *The Forest is Crying,* Hannibal Records HNCD 1342 (distributed by Rykodisc)

Vocal Traditions of Bulgaria, Saydisc CD/CSDL 396 (distributed by Harmonia Mundi)

Folk Music of Bulgaria, Topic TSCD 905

Useful addresses

The Embassy of the Republic of Bulgaria, 186/188 Queen's Gate SW7 5HL (tel: 0171-584 9400/9433)

Balkan Holidays London, Sofia House, 19 Conduit Street, London W1R 9TD (tel: 0171-491 4499)

The British–Bulgarian Friendship Society, Finsbury Library, 245 St Johns Street, London EC1V 4NB (tel: 0171-837 2304)

Hungary

Book list

Folksongs from Eastern Europe, Ken and Jean Bolam (Faber Music, 1992) (includes two Hungarian songs with English lyrics)

The following books of Hungarian folk-tales are available in English and Hungarian (bilingual) editions through the Hungarian Book Agency (see 'Useful addresses'):

The Three Wishes ('Granny's Storybooks')
The Silver King's Flute, Zsigmond Móricz
Palkó, the Piper, Elek Benedek

Most public libraries will hold Hungarian travel books and guides, many of which provide a useful source of good illustrations and interesting notes.

Recorded music

The Hungarian State Folk Ensemble, Monitor 51368 (includes Kalló double dance by Kodály based on folk material, wedding music and folk-songs and dances)
Hungarian Folk Music Sebö Ensemble, Rounder Records 5005 (Direct Distribution)
ARC Music has a number of listings of traditional music in its catalogue, including:
Famous Hungarian Gypsy Tunes EU/MC/CD 1133 (András Farkas, musician and composer, plays his own compositions, classical and traditional gypsy music)
Meta and the gypsy: Kálmán Balogh EU/MC/CD 1073 (Kálmán Balogh, one of the world's best cymbalom players, performs with Meta, one of Hungary's best folk groups)
Meta: Spring Breeze EU/MC/CD 1106 (typical spring songs showing well-known customs of European folklore in typical Hungarian variations; instruments include the cymbalom, tambourine, lute, flute with mouthpipe, Hungarian bagpipes, shepherd's pipe and shawm)

Classical music

Kodály: Háry János suite
Bartók: dance suite from The Wooden Prince, The Miraculous Mandarin, Mikrokosmos (piano pieces)
Liszt: Hungarian Rhapsodies (excerpts)

Useful addresses

Embassy of the Republic of Hungary, 35 Eaton Place, London SW1X 8BY (tel: 0171-235 4048)
Hungarian Folk Dance Group, c/o József Baracsi, 4 Chislehurst Avenue, London N12 0HU (tel: 0181-349 2474)
Hungarian Book Agency, 87 Sewardstone Road, London E2 9HN (tel: 0181-980 9096) (stocks books, maps, cards, records and cassettes)

Czech Republic

Book list

Folk Carols for Young Children, Barbara Cass-Beggs (Ward Lock Educational, 1980) (contains Czech carols: 'Rocking', 'From Beth'lem's City', 'Mary was watching', 'Hydom, hydom')
Folksongs from Eastern Europe, Ken and Jean Bolam (Faber Music, 1992) (includes seven Czech songs with English lyrics)
The following publications may still be available in libraries and resource centres:
Czechoslovakia: Children of the World, ed. Knowlton/ Wright (Gareth Stevens Childrens Books, 1989)
Let's Go To Czechoslovakia, Keith Lye (Franklin Watts, 1986)
Let's Visit Czechoslovakia, T. Popescu (Burke, 1983)
Most public libraries stock travel guides which have good illustrations and interesting notes.

Recorded music

The Oldest Collection of Czech Folk Songs, Supraphon 11 1293–2731
Bohemian Folk Songs, Supraphon 11 1592–2711
Folk Songs from Moravia, Supraphon 11 1511–2731
(All distributed by Koch International)

Classical music

Smetana: Ma Vlast ('My Fatherland')
Smetana: The Bartered Bride
Dvořák: Slavonic Dances
Dvořák: 'New World' Symphony
Janáček: Jenufa and *The Cunning Little Vixen*

Useful addresses

Embassy of the Czech Republic, 26 Kensington Palace Gardens, London W8 4QY (tel: 0171-243 1115)
Czech Centre, 95 Great Portland Street, London W1N 5RA (tel: 0171-291 9920)
(Provides information on cultural events and organizes exhibitions, concerts and lectures)

Germany

Book list

Focus on Germany and the Germans, Anita Ganeri (Watts, 1992)
Getting to know Germany and German, Janine Amos (Watts, 1992)
Germany: On the Map, David Flint (Wayland, 1993)
Germany: Country Fact Files, David Flint (Wayland, 1992)
Germany (from the 'Our Country' series), David Cumming (Wayland, 1993)
Germany (from the 'Countries of the World' series), David Cumming (Wayland, 1994)

Germany (from the 'Country Topics' series), R. Wright and T. Morris (Watts, 1993)

Look Inside Germany, Ian James/Joy Richardson (Watts, 1995)

Passport to Germany, Keith Lye (Franklin Watts, 1992)

First 1000 Words in German (Usborne, 1995)

German for Beginners: tape pack (Usborne, 1992)

First German At Home, At School, On Holiday (Usborne, 1993)

Food and Drink from Germany available from CMA UK (see Useful addresses)

Recorded music

HMV import direct from Germany. The following titles are representative of their selection of folk- and traditional music at the time of enquiry:

Concert Champêtre Tyrolien, ARN 64103 (local village brass band)

Münchner Biergarten Musikanten, JMP 3004020 (typical polkas and waltzes played for entertainment)

Auf Zum Oktoberfest Laser Light 79 055 (festival music, songs and intrumental)

Jodler und Schuhplattler, Koch 299 200 AB

HMV's main stock of world music is held at the HMV Shop, 150 Oxford Street, London W1N 0DJ. You can also telephone the HMV ORDERLINE 0171-637 1167 for specific items or an update.

Classical music

The range is enormous but here is a brief list to start with:

J. S. Bach: Toccata and Fugue in D Minor for Organ, 'Air on a G String' from Suite No. 3

Beethoven: Symphony No. 6 ('Pastoral'), Symphony No. 9 ('Choral')

Handel: 'Hallelujah' Chorus from *The Messiah*, Water Music

Mendelssohn: 'Hebrides' Overture, Overture to 'A Midsummer Night's Dream'

Carl Orff: Carmina Burana

Wagner: 'The Ride of the Valkyries' from *Die Walküre*

Useful addresses

Embassy of the Federal Republic of Germany, 23 Belgrave Square, London SW1X 8PZ (tel: 0171-824 1300)

German National Tourist Office, 65 Curzon Street, London W1Y 8PE (tel: 0891-600 100)

Goethe Institut, 50 Princes Gate, Exhibition Road, London SW7 2PH (tel: 0171-411 3400)

CMA UK, CMA House, 17A Church Road, London SW19 5DQ is the UK branch of the German Agricultural Marketing Board (tel: 0181-944 0484). School packs include recipe booklets, 'Food and Drink from Germany', posters, flags and decorations.

France

Book list

A Taste of France, Roz Denny (Wayland, 1994)

First Book of France, Louis Somerville (Usborne, 1993)

France (from the 'Countries of the World' series), Alan Blackwood (Wayland, 1991)

France: Country Fact Files, Daphne Butler (Wayland, 1994)

France (from the 'Country Topics' series), A. Ganeri and R. Wright (Watts, 1993)

France (from the 'Look Inside' series), Joy Richardson (Wayland, 1995)

Focus on France and the French, Anita Ganeri (Watts, 1994)

Getting to know France and French, Nicola Wright (Watts, 1993)

Passport to France, Dominique Norbrook (Watts, 1991)

First 1000 Words in French H. Amery (Usborne, 1995)

First French At Home, At School, On Holiday, K. Gemmell (Usborne, 1993)

French for Beginners (book and tape), A. Wilkes (Usborne, 1992)

Joan of Arc (from the 'Children of History' series), Brian Williams (Cherry Tree Books, 1989)

The French Revolution and Napoleon, Stephen Pratt (Wayland, 1992)

Recorded music

The following are distributed by Harmonia Mundi:

Hurdy Gurdy Music of Auvergne and Bourbonnais, Ocora CD C560007/MC 4560007 (includes hurdy-gurdy, bagpipes, accordion, clarinet; sleeve notes in English)

Songs of Lower Brittany, Ocora CD C559082/MC 4559082

Songs of Central Brittany, Ocora CD C559084/MC 4559084

French Accordion Music/Fleur du Jura, Saydisc CD-SDL353/MC CSDL353

The following are distributed by Discovery Records:

Dances de Bretagne, Keltia Musique KMCD 07

Breton Pipers, Keltia Musique KMCD 12

Sounds of Brittany, Keltia Musique KMCD 19

Folk Dances of Brittany Today, Keltia Musique KMCD 41 (played on traditional instruments)

Classical music

Berlioz: Symphonie Fantastique

Bizet: Toreador's Song from Carmen

Debussy: La mer ('The Sea') and piano pieces: 'Gardens in the Rain', 'The Submerged Cathedral', 'Goldfish'

Dukas: The Sorcerer's Apprentice

Ravel: Bolero, Mother Goose Suite, Pavan for a Dead Infanta

Saint-Saëns: Carnival of the Animals

Useful addresses

French Embassy (Cultural Counsellor), 23 Cromwell Road, London SW7 2DQ (tel: 0171-838 2055)
French Tourist Ofice, 179 Piccadilly, London W1V 0AL (tel: 0891-244 123)

Sweden

Book list

Sweden (from 'The Modern Industrial World' series), Bo Kage Carlsson (Wayland, 1995) (for older children or suitable as reference)
The Viking World, Philippa Wingate (Usborne, 1993)
Vikings (from the 'History Starters' series), Kath Davies (Zoë Books, 1995)
Vikings: Myths and Legends, Gilles Ragache (Cherry Tree Books, 1994)
Most public libraries stock travel guides which have good illustrations and interesting notes. Illustrated brochures can also be obtained from the Swedish Travel and Tourism Council (see 'Useful addresses').

Recorded music

Music of the Scandinavian Valleys, Ocora CD: C560008, and *Musiques Traditionnelles de Suède* AUVIDIS/SILEX Y 225215 (distributed by Harmonia Mundi)
Songs and Dances from Sweden, EU/MC/CD/1108 (distributed by ARC Music)
Svensk Folkmusik, Amalthea MNW 194/5 (distributed by Topic)

Useful addresses

Embassy of Sweden, 11 Montagu Place, London W1H 2AL (tel: 0171-724 2101)
The Swedish Church, 6 Harcourt Street, London W1H 1DS (tel: 0171-723 5681)
The Swedish Travel and Tourism Council, 11 Montagu Place, London W1H 2AL (tel: 0171-724 5868)

May Day

Book list

Festivals, Ruth Manning-Sanders (Heinemann, 1972) (includes a section on May Day and the Padstow 'Obby Oss')

Spring Festivals, Summer Festivals, Mike Rosen (Wayland, 1990)
English Traditional Dancing in the National Curriculum, Wendy Crouch (English Folk Dance and Song Society, 1996) (book and cassette)
Baskets and Banana Skins - a new approach to the teaching of country dancing (NC Key Stages 2/3), Richard Stapledon (John Bull Music 1995) available from John Bull Music, 81 Main Street, Thringstone, Leicestershire LE6 4ND (book and cassette)
May: An educational resource pack for the Summer Term on British traditions, Education Resource Pack No. 1 (English Folk Dance and Song Society, 1993)

Recorded music

All Round England and Back Again, Saydisc CSDL332 (includes recordings from Helston of the Furry Dance and Hal-an-tow and from Padstow of the Hobby Horse Day, available from The Folk Shop at Cecil Sharp House (see 'Useful addresses'); full listings include folk songs and dances from all over the UK; write for a catalogue.

Classical music

Percy Grainger: Shepherd's Hey; English Dance; Mock Morris
Vaughan Williams: Fantasia on Greensleeves; Pastoral Symphony; English Folk Song Suite

Useful addresses

The English Folk Dance and Song Society, Cecil Sharp House, 2 Regent's Park Road, London NW1 7AY (tel: 0171-485 2206)
The EFDSS is the main centre for information and material to do with English folk song, dance and traditions. It has a well-stocked shop containing books, music, records and instruments (tel: 0171 284 0534) and an extensive library (tel: 0171 284 0523).
Carolyn Robson, former EFDSS education officer, runs school workshops incorporating traditional dance and other folk arts into the curiculum (tel: 01252 722 938).